CURSED IN NEW YORK

STORIES OF THE DAMNED IN THE EMPIRE STATE

Randi Minetor

Globe
Pequot

GUILFORD, CONNECTICUT
An imprint of Rowman & Littlefield

Globe
Pequot

An imprint of Rowman & Littlefield

Distributed by NATIONAL BOOK NETWORK

ISBN 978-1-4930-1376-0 (paperback)

978-1-4930-1377-7 (ebook)

British Library Cataloguing in Publication Information Available

Library of Congress Cataloging-in-Publication Data

Minetor, Randi.
 Cursed in New York : stories of the damned in the Empire State / Randi Minetor.
   pages cm
  Includes bibliographical references and index.
  ISBN 978-1-4930-1376-0 (paperback : alkaline paper) – ISBN 978-1-4930-1377-7 (electronic) 1. Blessing and cursing–New York (State)–Anecdotes. 2. Revenge–New York (State)–Anecdotes. 3. Evil eye–New York (State)–Anecdotes.
4. Damned–New York (State)–Biography–Anecdotes. 5. Legends–New York (State) 6. Tales–New York (State) 7. New York (State)–Social life and customs–Anecdotes. 8. New York (State)–Biography–Anecdotes. I. Title.
  GR110.N7M56 2015
  398.209747–dc23   2015017576

∞™ The paper used in this publication meets the minimum requirements of American National Standard for Information Sciences–Permanence of Paper for Printed Library Materials, ANSI/NISO Z39.48-1992.

CURSED IN NEW YORK

CONTENTS

PREFACE

The stories you are about to read are based on oral history, folklore, written accounts, and—in many cases—actual fact. In approaching the question of cursed people, objects, and places, I have endeavored to use my skills as a researcher to rout out the facts among the tales of mayhem and malevolence, if facts could be found. I followed the words of the famous Russian proverb: *Doveryai, no proveryai* (or, in English, "Trust, but verify"). When I could find no verification, I chose not to tell that story.

It is not my intention to spoil the fun of these tales, nor am I totally convinced that these stories can and should be debunked. I simply searched for truth, wherever it may hide. In some cases, it became impossible to deny that a person cursed by an adversary came to harm, or that an individual who owned a cursed object suffered dire consequences. I make no attempt to determine how such a thing could take place; I am only a humble reporter, not a medium, mystic, scientist, or priest.

In reading this book, I caution you to heed the words of William Shakespeare: "There are more things in heaven and earth, Horatio, than are dreamt of in your philosophy." Evil may lurk, but not all that lurks is evil. Read on.

INTRODUCTION

"**O**y, ken-a-hora!"

My mother said this frequently when I was a child, almost always after someone gave me a compliment. It wasn't until I began work on this book that I learned the phrase was meant to protect me, in that backhanded way that comes from the impassioned cultures of Eastern Europe. *Ken-a-hora* (or, more precisely, *kein ayin hara*) is a Yiddish expression that translates to "There should be no evil eye!"

What is the evil eye, and why should a compliment draw its attention? As I researched this book, I came across dozens of variations on the concept. For Jews—like my mother—any compliment is an invitation to *ein hara*, the evil eye, to take that good fortune away from people so bold as to believe that they deserve this goodness.

Thus, the compliment becomes a curse. That's the kind of perverse logic that has haunted me since childhood . . . and, as it turns out, it's not far from the beliefs of just about every culture on earth.

In the Middle East, people in Afghanistan, Iran, Greece, and Turkey hang talismans in their homes to ward off *Isabat al-'ayn*, their belief that a person or animal only has to look at them to curse their very existence. Hindus fear *Drishti* (also known as *Buri Nazar*) and decorate their babies' eyes with black eyeliner to ward off this spirit of evil. In Ethiopia, some Christians of different social groups believe that other groups can hurl the power of *bouda* at them, so they carry amulets to keep this force from destroying their happiness.

Pakistani truck drivers ward off the evil eye by placing squares of black cloth on their bumpers to keep them safe while driving. In Greece, fear of the evil eye leads to secretive rituals passed down within families, involving prayers that must be revealed to the younger generation by their grandparents when a time of potential distress is close at hand. The Italian belief in *malocchio* is so ingrained in the culture that I devoted a whole chapter to it in this book.

All these forces of evil have one thing in common: They can be inflicted by a word, a gesture, or a glance. Anyone who has the power—essentially, anyone who wishes you ill—can curse you simply by telling you that they have done so.

This makes a curse a frightening thing indeed. By definition, a curse implies that someone (or something) *intends* that you should suffer harm. This intent is the key element that makes a curse different from other visitations from the hoary netherworld—like, for example, a haunting.

When I began this research, many people wanted to tell me all about the ghosts that inhabited their homes or property, or that drifted about in old buildings throughout the state. Let me say that, for the purposes of this book, it makes no difference whether I personally believe in ghosts; many people do, and they are certain that these sylphs haunt places all over the state in great numbers. I looked into some of these stories, and the staggering level of documentation of these apparitions certainly speaks to their popularity. Only one or two of the ghosts seemed to wish anyone evil, however, and only a handful of them had evil done to them during their days as corporeal beings. In this book, you will find some tales of spirits condemned to spend their metaphysical existence in the buildings in which they lived in life. This is not a book of hauntings and ghost stories, however, and I hope this fact will not discourage you from reading further.

Instead, most of the legends selected for *Cursed in New York* happened to people here in our great state who felt the impact of the curses during their lives. In some cases, the curse led them to rack and ruin—in fact, some curses actually drove people to take their own lives, most often with great drama. The sequential ownership of one gemstone, in fact, made three people leap off of tall buildings to die on the pavement below. With numbers and coincidental events like that, it's hard to argue that no malevolent force was involved.

Here's the other thing that makes curses so terrifying: Anyone, it seems, can curse another human being. The act requires no special powers or previous experience. It may be that a curse only takes effect if the person doing the cursing truly and deeply wishes bad luck on the person being cursed. Perhaps, for example, the lack of heartless ill will kept Ann Cooper Clarke's curse on her children at Hyde Hall from having the deleterious effect she intended (see chapter 15).

If you are on the receiving end of the curse, you may not even realize that you did something wrong. You could simply be doing your job, like Alexander Hamilton and Aaron Burr when they defended a young man accused of murdering a young Quaker woman in 1802. It's the law of the land that every person accused of a crime is entitled to a competent defense . . . but when these two distinguished gentlemen did what the law told them to do, they got a curse for their troubles. Every student of history knows how this one ended (and if you don't, you can find out in chapter 12).

You might just swim in the wrong lake, like the hapless young men who took a dip in Lake Ronkonkoma on Long Island and found themselves in deep, dark waters determined (if a lake can be determined) to avenge an Indian princess. Or you might root for a sports team that betrayed a promise to a former coach, or one that happens to be in the same city where a president of the United States met an untimely end. Either way, you are doomed to one season of disappointment after another.

What did any of these people do to deserve their fates? For the most part, they showed up in the wrong place at the right time. They bought a property where a murder had taken place, constructed a building on the site of an ancient burial ground, purchased a gem stolen from an east Indian temple, intruded on a spirit in a cave, or spent their last days separated from their loved ones because of a state law. Some of these people knew that their actions could bring the wrath of evil down upon them, but most made an innocent misstep. Now, decades or centuries later, we still speak and write about the results.

This book contains stories collected from across New York State, from the eastern reaches of Long Island to the gorges of Niagara Falls. Here you'll find tales documented by reputable sources ranging from the *New York Times* to the Associated Press, as well as some that make a tissue of half-truths and long-forgotten sources surprisingly substantial and plausible.

As you read these tales, I offer these words of advice, based on parallels I have drawn as I completed my research. First, keep in mind that if you believe you are cursed, then you very certainly are. This may be why so many of these stories go in such a direction of misfortune, often over the course of many years. The power of suggestion may be one of the strongest in the human mind, reinforcing itself as more and more evidence mounts to turn an idea into a reality. So, for example, a team that feels the weight of six different kinds of curses can't help but continue to have one losing season after another.

And second, watch out for the logical fallacy *post hoc ergo propter hoc*, or the reasoning that if a person did A, and then B happened, A caused B. It's easy enough to believe that a curse caused bad things to happen, especially in retrospect—and we often go looking for reasons when we cannot accept the randomness of bad fortune. Not all of life's difficulties offer us someone or something to blame, and not all things happen for a reason.

That being said, when someone stands in front of you, points a finger at you, and says, "I curse you and your household! May no one ever see a day of happiness here!" it can be tough to believe that any strife you experience from that day forward is *not* a result of this curse.

To this, I say, *"Ken-a-hora!"* I invite you to read about the misfortunes of others, and thank your lucky stars that none of these things are happening to you.

1

ANCIENT,
UNSPORTSMANLIKE
SOULS

Why haven't the Buffalo Bills won a football championship game since 1965?

Every beleaguered fan from the shores of Lake Erie to the central Pennsylvania border has a response to this question: player shenanigans, faults on the field, a home in a shrinking city, or too much turmoil at the top of the organization. Buffalo residents who live in this "drinking town with a sports problem," however, may be missing a barely noticed nugget of information about the Bills—not about the team itself, but about where it plays the game.

Journalist Aaron Lowinger dug up a story for the *Buffalo Spree* in 2012 that points to a curse, one rising out of the very ground on which Ralph Wilson Stadium was constructed (it was Rich Stadium then) back in 1973.

If you've been to the stadium, you may have felt the chilling winds that blow off of Lake Erie and whip through the stands, driving even the hardiest Bills fans to zip their parkas up to their noses. The unnatural cold—even for Buffalo—may be one more sign of the sinister and ghostly forces that keep western New York's team from the long overdue winning streak its fans deserve.

According to Lowinger's dogged research, Ralph Wilson Stadium sits on hallowed ground: a Native American settlement long since lost to the bloody, brutal Iroquois Wars of the 1600s, and then to the European settlers who followed them.

You may never have heard of the Wenrohronon people, but they were one of the tribal groups who lived in western New York in the sixteenth and seventeenth centuries. The Wenrohronon (shortened to Wenro by historians) maintained a tenuous peace with the Seneca, the Erie, and another little-known tribe, the Neutrals, with whom they shared land and trade. Eventually, the smaller tribes fell to the larger as the Iroquois swept through this area, and the Wenro were absorbed into the Six Nations of the Iroquois. They left behind a village built here on the banks of Smoke Creek, and they buried their dead along the outskirts of the village.

How can we know that Native Americans were laid to rest here? For this information, we turn to the legendary Arthur C. Parker, director of the Rochester Museum and Science Center from 1925 to 1945, and a recognized authority on American Indian culture. Born on a Seneca reservation and part Seneca himself, Parker took an active interest in the heritage of the Iroquois people. His position as first archaeologist with the New York State Museum gave him the opportunity to create an atlas of places throughout the state where Native American artifacts had been discovered.

In his 1920 atlas, Parker describes the exact site on which the stadium would be built decades later: "Village site, extensive, in East Hamburg at the junction of Smokes Creek and a small brook. The site is on the George Ellis and Charles Diemer farm east of Abbott Road. The occupation is identified by Professor Houghton [another archaeologist working on the atlas] as Wenro. A large cemetery was destroyed by contractors and many clay vessels were broken and thrown in excavation."

And that, my friends—in the hands of careless construction workers predating the formation of Buffalo's team by four decades or more—is when the Bills' trouble began.

WHERE NOT TO BUILD

Horror movies of the late twentieth century provide us with some of the best advice we could want for avoiding the effects of the supernatural: Don't go in the basement, don't go in the attic, don't go in the woods . . . and for the love of God, don't build your home—or stadium, for our purposes—on the site of an ancient Indian burial ground.

The trope has become so familiar that every animated television series from *The Simpsons* to *Family Guy* has spoofed it. Bloggers and tweeters even have an acronym for it: Indian burial ground is IBG.

Why are these ancient cemeteries so scary and threatening? Disturbing the last resting place of anyone's bones certainly has an innate creepiness, but when these bones come from the native peoples of our great land, their removal literally adds insult to injury. Dr. Lawrence Rosen of Princeton University explained this in a paper published in *American Anthropologist*: "The excavation of Indian burial sites poses serious ethical problems. Many American Indians regard the excavation of such sites as an affront to their actual and spiritual ancestors." He goes on to note that anthropologists feel that digging up Indian bones is indispensible to their research, giving them clues to the relationship between diet, disease, ecology, and social strata and how they affect all human beings. These pursuits fly in the faces of Native Americans, however, who "trace their actual descent or spiritual affiliation to ancestors whose graves, in their view, are disturbed in the name of dispassionate science. To many Indians, the disinterment or display of Indian skeletons is an indignity that most scientists would hesitate to inflict on their own predecessors."

If digging up graves in the name of science is a horrendous insult to the Native American culture, how can they possibly feel about the location of their ancestors' remains becoming a football field?

The laws of our state keep the descendants of these ancient people from retaliating against those who destroyed the graves and threw their relics willy-nilly, but there's no law in America to keep the spirits of these irritated ancestors from taking matters into their own hands.

Iroquois legends describe the inhabitants of the Spirit World as gentle souls living on a beautiful island where flowers bloom and spring is eternal. The idea that these spirits might take on malevolent powers and seek revenge comes from a European sensibility, one that created a concept of a dark underworld that can produce phantoms who perform black magic.

Combine this with a fairly recent change in sensibilities—the grim acknowledgment of the injustices done to America's native peoples since the 1600s—and we have a veritable stew of guilt, fear, and helplessness that leads us to a single conclusion: Indians are cursing us from beyond the shattered grave.

MORE FUEL FOR THE FIRE

The Bills are not the only team to suffer the affliction brought on by co-locating with long-dead Native Americans.

The Miami Dolphins play in Sun Life Stadium, constructed on the ninth-century burial site of the Tequesta tribe, who inhabited the shores of Biscayne Bay until the Europeans arrived in the sixteenth century. The conquering Spaniards passed their diseases on to the Native Americans and all but wiped them out entirely by the 1700s, leaving nothing but the graves discovered when the Dolphins broke ground on the stadium in 1985. This time the contractors called in archaeologists and had the site excavated properly and respectfully, but fans can't help but notice that the once-champion Dolphins have not been to the Super Bowl since the Native American remains were exhumed.

In Chicago, evidence of a Native American burial ground was discovered just a few blocks from Wrigley Field, the ballpark built in 1914, where the Chicago Cubs have never won a championship. Frustrated fans speculate that the burial site may have extended to the land beneath the field, preceding the Theological Seminary of the Evangelical Church of America, which stood here for two decades before it was torn down to make way for Wrigley.

Are these nothing more than convenient excuses for one loss after another? Are urban legends catching up with reality? Or could there be some truth to the notion that long-dead Native Americans are making our professional sports teams lose?

To find some kind of answer to this discouraging phenomenon, let's take a quick trip to Long Island to find out how this curse of the ancients became so prevalent in twentieth-century pop culture.

YOU GUESSED IT: AMITYVILLE

Long before it became so clichéd that it crossed over into comedy, disturbing the Native Americans' final resting place served as the reason for the hauntings in Amityville, New York, in the home that became the subject of 1977 book and 1979 film *The Amityville Horror*.

The story of the haunted house sprang from the very real 1974 murder case of twenty-three-year-old Ronald DeFeo Jr., who killed his parents and four siblings in their home at 112 Ocean Avenue. As improbable as it may seem, someone bought the house in December 1975: George and Kathy Lutz, who moved in with their three children, fully cognizant of the gruesome acts that had taken place there. Twenty-eight days later, they moved out—and their tale of the paranormal activity that drove them from the house became the subject of an astonishingly successful book.

The Lutzes described swarms of flies, strange smells, visions of a pig-person with glowing red eyes, slime oozing from the walls, spontaneous levitation, voices telling them to "Get out!" and a good deal more. These supernatural events were the result of more than the grisly murders, the book claimed: The sturdy Dutch colonial had been built on a Shinnecock Indian graveyard—and not just any graveyard, but one that served an Indian sanitarium, where the dying would be left to perish outdoors in the cold and dark of a New York winter. The spirits of these twice-afflicted people inhabited the house, providing the voices that Ronald DeFeo heard telling him to murder everyone in his family.

Shinnecocks in Amityville? The mention of this tribe stirred a number of debunkers into action, not the least of which was the Montaukett Nation, the Native Americans who actually lived—and still live—in the Amityville area. The Montauketts have been clear that the Shinnecocks never resided in this part of Long Island, and there was no burial ground or sanitarium on this spot. They went so far as to take author and criminologist Ric Osuna, writer of the debunking manifesto *The Night the DeFeos Died*, on a tour of the real Indian burial grounds in this part of Long Island, most of which now serve as dumps. To their knowledge, none of these have produced creepy hauntings or long decades of bad luck for the residents in proximity.

The misidentification of the local Native Americans was just one of the many clues that the tale of 112 Ocean Avenue was a work of fiction. Eventually, Ronald DeFeo's defense attorney, William Weber, owned up in an interview with *People* magazine to helping the Lutzes create the crazy story to net a massive book deal. He then sued them when they took the concept and made a deal that excluded him.

No steaming pile of truth, however, kept the *Amityville Horror* franchise from building its own momentum. Today no fewer than eleven additional movies (many of them direct-to-DVD) have been made, a testament to the success of the disturbed Indian burial ground as being a very scary place.

Just down the road from Amityville, the IBG served again in the 1982 film *Poltergeist* (which no one claimed to be factual)—another suburban Long Island home disrupted by Native Americans who could no longer rest beneath it. Stephen King used the native burial ground in his 1983 novel, *Pet Sematary*, which became a movie in 1989. *Blood Trail, Dark Harvest, Skeleton Man, Terror at Tate Manor, Death4Told, The Haunted, The Reptile* . . . the list of movies that pivot on an Indian burial ground continues to grow, giving weight to the idea that unseen forces below ground can continue to torment us, especially if they happen to have arrived on this continent long before we European, Asian, or African descendants did.

Since 1990, any unearthed Native American remains are protected by the federal Native American Graves Protection and Repatriation Act, which gives the excavators strict instructions to return the remains to the Native American organization in question. Perhaps this will help keep new stories of haunted, hallowed ground from creeping into newly constructed housing tracts. But it's the older homes, the Dutch colonial with the eerie look of a jack-o'-lantern or the three-story Italianate mansion with the drafty attic and the square cupola, that become the receptacles for ghostly tales of restless natives.

2

THE INDIAN PRINCESS OF LAKE RONKONKOMA

A legend tells the story of
A pretty Indian maid
Who loved a handsome pale-faced lad
But marriage was forbade.
Her father chose another mate
A fine strong Indian brave.
The Indian girl could not comply
And so her life she gave.
Ronkonkoma Ronkonkoma
The lake of sparkling water.
Ronkonkoma Ronkonkoma
Where rests the Indian daughter.

—Lois J. Watt

Of all the stories of lovers forced apart by their parents, by an accident of birth, or by dreadful circumstance, few wrap themselves around the heart as completely as the tale of Ronkonkoma (pronounced ron-*kon*-ko-ma), the Indian princess who cursed the lake that bears her name.

Her story stirs more sorrow than fear, because she means no harm in pulling young men down into the deep waters of this freshwater lake. Ronkonkoma simply hopes to find a lover who can take the place of her first and most passionate love: a white settler named Hugh Birdsall, who lived across the lake from Ronkonkoma's tribe and never sought to bewitch the beautiful princess with his affections. No, Ronkonkoma sought him, spotting Birdsall while he was cutting wood in the forest and falling instantly in love with the handsome young man.

It's a story that grows more relevant with each passing year, one that combines elements of race, distance, raw emotion, and the ultimate tragic end—and its consequences are felt even today, as another life ends each summer and residents are left to ponder the causes.

But we are already ahead of ourselves in telling this tale. First, let's understand exactly where this seventeenth-century romantic tragedy took place, and why these two lovers became entangled there.

THE BOTTOMLESS LAKE

If mapmakers were to pinpoint the center of Long Island, north to south and east to west, their markers would fall quite close to Lake Ronkonkoma. The lake can be found just north of the Long Island Expressway at the end of Pond Road, off of the highway's exit 59, where it provides residents and tourists with a tranquil place to swim, fish, canoe, and kayak in the midsummer sun.

Fresh, beautiful, and filled with aquatic life, the lake has attracted human settlement for hundreds of years. Four Indian tribes established their homes here first: the Nissequogues, Secatogs, Unkechaugs, and the Setalcotts, also known as the Setaukets (for whom the North Shore town of Setauket would be named in the 1600s). These first peoples represented four of the thirteen tribes of Long Island. The Setaukets were a particularly powerful tribe among the thirteen, and it is from this tribe that the legend of the Indian princess of Lake Ronkonkoma springs.

On the shores of this lake, one the native people held most sacred, the Setaukets and their counterparts carried out their worshipful rituals under the watchful eye of the Great Spirit. It would be easy to assume that they gathered around this lake because of the abundance of food it must contain, but these first Long Islanders believed that the lake's waters protected fish and other marine life within them, so they did not disturb their aquatic neighbors. This posed no problem, however, as the surrounding lands provided all the food they needed, allowing the Setaukets to leave the lake just as they found it.

Beyond its mysteries as a sacred place, Lake Ronkonkoma held other secrets in its depths. Its floor descends into darkness, a churned-silt murkiness so deep that both Indian and European settlers determined that it must be bottomless. Natives told stories of their brothers drowning in the depths of the lake and their bodies disappearing forever, never floating to the surface. Others claimed that the bodies would turn up miles from the lake, drifting on waterways that emptied into the Great South Bay, the forty-five-mile-long lagoon between Long Island and Fire Island. In the 1700s, witnesses watched as a white man dropped a weight on a string over the side of his boat into the deepest part of the lake and played out the entire length of his line—some accountings of this legend say for a thousand feet or more—without encountering the bottom.

None of these early residents could know, of course, what a federal government study would determine in the twentieth century: Lake Ronkonkoma is a natural well, filling itself with fresh water from the underground water table and, essentially, controlling its own depth as the rush of clear water flows into and out of its lower extremities. Formed by a glacier that scooped out the lakebed and drilled itself deep into the ground, the lake connects to its hidden water source toward Ronkonkoma's southern end. Modern science calculates that the deepest parts of Lake Ronkonkoma—two chasms at the southern end of the lake—bottom out at sixty-five feet and ninety-two feet. This is hardly bottomless, but these two plunge points come as a sheer drop-off from a ledge at a depth of only about fifteen feet. If you were caught by the drop and plunged into sudden, underwater darkness, the depth would indeed seem endless.

The behavior of this hole also may explain the belief that a whirl-pool forms in the middle of the lake, one strong enough to capture a canoe and its passengers and pull them downward. Modern science tells us that there is no force within the lake that could create such a phenomenon, but it also tells us that objects disappearing into the lake could not possibly find their way into waterways miles away, nor could the bodies of drowning victims escape discovery for months and suddenly surface elsewhere . . . and yet they do.

So Lake Ronkonkoma offers more than its fair share of mysteries, only some of which can be explained away by geology. Herein lies the story of the Indian princess, a lovely lass who would breathe her last and descend into the darkest waters of the lake that now bears her name. And herein also lie the many victims who have fallen in the princess's search for a lover to match her beloved seventeenth-century woodcutter, the enigmatic Hugh Birdsall.

THE LADY OF THE LAKE

Ronkonkoma (some accounts call her Tuskawanta, by the way) was the daughter of the chief of the Setauket tribe, a position that obligated her to marry a man selected from among her tribesmen. An adventurous soul with a curious spirit, she often followed paths in the forest along the lake to explore the land on which neighboring tribes lived.

On one of her trips, she spotted one of the white settlers, a man in the first party of explorers who found their way from the tip of Long Island to this quiet lake. Ronkonkoma hid in the woods to watch as this handsome woodcutter chopped logs he might use to build structures or heat a cabin.

The attractive stranger with the light skin lived on the banks of the nearby Connetquot River, where he constructed a hut from the wood he harvested. Ronkonkoma came to watch him night after night, being careful to keep herself hidden. She knew that her behavior was forbidden in her tribe—her father would be very angry to know that she ventured so close to the new settlers, and all the more so if he guessed her interest in this young man.

Finally, on a moonlit night, the woodcutter could not sleep. He opened his door and went outside to pace in front of his cabin. A flash of bright light in the woods caught his eye, interrupting his reverie—a reflection of the glass beads Ronkonkoma wore. The young man dashed to the edge of the woods and discovered the beautiful Indian princess.

What happened next is lost to history, but soon Ronkonkoma and her woodcutter, Hugh Birdsall, fell in love. Ronkonkoma knew that she would face her father's anger and the scorn of her people if she pursued such a relationship, but love often conquers fear of family rejection. She decided to confront her father and demand to be married to the man across the lake.

Her father would have none of it. He forbade Ronkonkoma to see Birdsall ever again, forcing her to marry the Setauket man selected for her through the guidance of the Great Spirit.

For seven long years, Ronkonkoma and Birdsall continued their love affair through messages the Indian princess sent to the wood-cutter across the lake. Every day, Ronkonkoma paddled her canoe to the center of the lake, setting adrift a piece of bark with a message for the man she loved. Birdsall waited at the edge of the lake for the treasured scrap of bark to arrive, knowing that his lover would find a way to communicate with him day after day, month after month . . . year after year, for seven long years.

In the last month of the seventh year, Ronkonkoma could no longer stand this long-distance love. The legends differ on exactly what the Indian princess did next, but they all agree on one thing: Despair overcame her, and she took her own life.

One tale tells of a message the princess sent to Birdsall, telling him she would finally join him the next morning. As the woodcutter waited by the water, Ronkonkoma's seemingly empty canoe came down the Connetquot River to his cabin. Inside, he found his Indian lover with a knife blade through her heart.

Another suggests that Ronkonkoma tried to swim across the lake to Birdsall and his cabin, but the distance of just over a kilometer (about two-thirds of a mile) proved to be too much for her, and she drowned in a deep part of the lake. In a third version, Ronkonkoma sent a message asking Birdsall to meet her in the middle of the lake, but when he did not come, she committed the final, hopeless act of drowning herself.

To this day, the legend tells us, Ronkonkoma continues to search for her dearest Hugh Birdsall. Once a year, she chooses a man roughly between the ages of eighteen and forty and takes him down into the depths of the lake to live with her for eternity. As she will never find her true lover, the drowning victims will continue to mount up until she finds an equivalent match who satisfies her need for love.

HERE'S WHERE THE STORY GETS CREEPY

It's easy enough to scoff at a legend that pits a long-dead seventeenth-century princess against the skills and equipment of modern-day lifeguards on a public beach . . . until you start doing the math.

While there are not many public records about drowning deaths in Lake Ronkonkoma before the 1950s, quite a number of these accidental deaths have taken place since 1965. These are detailed in a book by David Igneri, a lifeguard who worked the waters of Lake Ronkonkoma from 1965 until 1994.

Igneri and his staff made hundreds of heroic rescues on the lake in those thirty years, maintaining a perfect record with no deaths in the protected beach area. Every year, however, one person would slip through their grasp, drowning in a part of the lake beyond the designated lifeguard area. Every year, that person was a male in the age range the Indian princess finds most desirable: somewhere between the ages of eighteen and forty.

Igneri took these deaths very personally, as he wrote in his book, *Lake Ronkonkoma in History and Legend, the Princess, Curse, and Other Stories: A Lifeguard's View.* Of one rescue, he wrote, "The Princess . . . had taken young males, all over the lake, for over a century. Now the legend had stopped at the protected beach, on the south side of the lake. She decided she would take her next victim, on my beach at Lake Ronkonkoma. To play it safe she would take her victim, after the lifeguards had left. She wanted to totally humiliate (yours truly), for having stopped so many of the drownings she had tried, over the many years. To make matters worse, she would make sure I was at Lake Ronkonkoma swimming, but too far away to make the rescue."

The princess failed to take the particular victim Igneri describes here, but the lifeguard gives detailed accounts of a number of drownings, all of them involving men who chose to swim outside of the designated safe and guarded part of the lake. In one case, a man came to the lake to swim, but the beach was closed because of pollution. The man chose to swim in an unprotected area far from lifeguards and drowned in "about forty-five feet of water," according to Igneri. "I felt very bad about this drowning," he continued. "I had spoken to him only hours before his death."

Then, in 2000—six years after Igneri's departure—drowning ceased to take any more victims for eleven years. Perhaps the Indian princess had finally found a man who resembled the dashing Hugh Birdsall, or perhaps she had developed a sense of fairness and mercy that exceeded her need to reunite with her lover. Whatever the mystical cause, no more young men met their maker in the waters of the lake until 2012, when Sammie Weiner, a father of two children, went into the water to retrieve a remote-controlled boat for a stranger on the shore at about 8:30 p.m. on Friday, June 22. He swam out about 150 feet, then suddenly vanished underwater and never surfaced. His body was found the following evening after an exhaustive search of the lake, close to where he had gone under.

No drowning was recorded in 2013, but on August 23, 2014, the body of kayaker Kevin Conley, age forty, finally emerged after a nine-day search that included divers and sonar to penetrate the "zero visibility" area of the lake. Conley had fallen out of his canoe in a particularly murky part of the lake, which masked his location for more than a week.

Whether or not the lady of the lake will continue to claim victims remains to be seen, but every new death gives more credence to a legend that has endured for more than four hundred years. If you are male, between the ages of eighteen and forty, and a resident of Long Island, I can only suggest this: Go and admire Lake Ronkonkoma if you must, but think twice before you swim in it. A ghostly princess may mistake you for a very attractive and virile woodcutter.

3

The Truth about Shakespeare's Scottish Play

Whether you're a professional actor or technician, a community theater stagehand, a Broadway scenic designer, or a high school chorister, you share one ironclad belief with all other thespians around the globe: Whispering the name "Macbeth" backstage will lead to disaster.

So strong is this particular belief that the very mention of the name in any setting—the middle of a crowded mall, a desert wilderness, or the comfort of your living room—can spook some theater veterans into knocking on wood, spitting between two fingers, or crying, "Toi, toi, toi!" Most theater professionals refer to the classic piece only as "The Scottish Play," or "Mackers" in Canada, fearing to utter the full name either inside or outside of a performance hall.

Macbeth, of course, is the title character in William Shakespeare's extraordinary play, *The Tragedy of Macbeth*, the story of a military general whose lust for power so overwhelms him that he murders his own king to create a path to the throne for himself. This act of violence proves to be only the first of many as Macbeth—spurred on by his wife, who may be even more ambitious than he—orders the murder of a series of noblemen, eventually including the wife and children of landowner Macduff, whom Macbeth believes stand in his way. Remorse eventually overtakes the general, however, as Lady Macbeth commits suicide to escape her own guilt and Macbeth himself realizes that he faces the rest of his life—"tomorrow and to-morrow and tomorrow"—alone with his regrets. The ill-fated Macbeth submits to the prophecy foretold by a trio of witches, deciding not to resist the vengeful Macduff's final attack.

Many plays tell convoluted tales of murder, conspiracy, and dark passion, so what makes *Macbeth* such a focus of fear and dread? Strangely enough, productions of this play have been fraught with a wide range of perils, from a reported ban by King James I to broken bones, fatal illnesses, and even death by stabbing. While some claim that there have actually been more accidents and deaths in productions of *Hamlet*—another Shakespeare masterpiece—than *Macbeth*, the certainty that the Scottish Play carries its own curse has led to a comprehensive cataloging of incidents during its productions. *Macbeth* has proved itself over and over again to be a dangerous play to rehearse and perform, whether the hazard comes from the choreographed battles with heavy, clumsy broadswords, the complex staging many theaters take on to present this common repertory staple in an original way . . . or the specter of supernatural forces that swarm to activate the play's inherent evils.

The story goes that Shakespeare, in an effort to impress King James I of England, not only set *Macbeth* in the king's native Scotland but also chose to pander to the monarch's personal fascination with witchcraft. Act IV begins with three witches—the ones who prophesied Macbeth's rise to power in Act I—tossing sinister ingredients into a boiling cauldron:

> *Double, double, toil and trouble;*
> *Fire burn, and cauldron bubble.*
> *Fillet of a fenny snake,*
> *In the cauldron boil and bake;*
> *Eye of newt and toe of frog,*
> *Wool of bat and tongue of dog,*
> *Adder's fork and blind-worm's sting,*
> *Lizard's leg and howlet's wing,*
> *For a charm of powerful trouble,*
> *Like a hell-broth boil and bubble.*

... and so on. To the twenty-first-century ear, these words sound like finely crafted poetry. To the purveyors of witchcraft in 1606, however, this was a closely guarded incantation that the playwright had dared to copy verbatim into his manuscript.

Why would Shakespeare do such a thing? Apparently King James I was himself a crusader against the dark arts, and he had written his own book, *Daemonologie*, railing against the black magic practiced by the witches of the day. Shakespeare sought to impress the king by using this book as a reference for his play. (This, by the way, is the same King James I for whom the so-named English translation of the Bible was written.)

Instead, middle-aged Will brought the wrath of the witches of London down upon his play. The witches, hearing of this affront to their sacred ritual, cursed the play outright for all eternity—a curse that we see play out over and over again in an alarming number of productions of *The Tragedy of Macbeth*.

The story differs a bit in some versions. According to another, more obscure legend, the original property master couldn't find an appropriate cauldron to use onstage, so he pilfered one from an actual witches' coven. The witches retaliated by cursing the play itself forever.

To top off the insults to Shakespeare's work, King James didn't even like it—in fact, he disliked the play so intensely that he banned further productions of it for five years.

Like any other banned book, *Macbeth*'s controversial reputation only made it more attractive to other directors and theater troupes. By the late 1600s, the play had become a popular repertory piece and a crowd-pleaser in theaters throughout Europe. This popularity added a new layer to its notoriety, however: When a theater company did not draw the desired houses to whatever play they had mounted, they often closed that play abruptly and pulled the company's greatest success, *Macbeth*, out of repertoire to replace the money-losing flop. Hearing the Scottish Play quoted backstage meant that someone was rehearsing his lines for the upcoming remounting of the repertory production—which meant that the actors in the failed play were about to be out of a job. Lines from *Macbeth* became such a powerful synonym for bad luck that actors began to treat the phenomenon as if it were the evil eye.

If a witch's curse and a warning of unemployment were not enough on their own to make theater professionals wary of *Macbeth*, the growing record of onstage and backstage accidents put the play's supernatural malevolence over the top. In that first production that King James hated so much, Hal Berridge, the young man playing Lady Macbeth, became sick with a fever and actually died, and legend has it that Shakespeare himself stepped into the role. In 1672, the actor in the title role replaced a blunt stage dagger with a real one, taking the life of the actor who played Duncan—right in front of a live audience. In some tales, the curse even extends to those reading a copy of the play: On April 9, 1865, just a week before his assassination by actor John Wilkes Booth, President Abraham Lincoln took a copy of *Macbeth* with him on a cruise on the Potomac River.

Accidents, injuries, and illnesses haunted productions through the centuries as *Macbeth* crossed the Atlantic Ocean and arrived in America. New York City welcomed two productions of the play in 1849 . . . and penned a new chapter in the legend of a curse.

RIOT ON ASTOR PLACE

There was a time in the history of the American theater when the audience's passion for one actor or another could actually incite a riot between the two rival factions. In the Manhattan of the mid-nineteenth century, such a conflict played right into another serious rift between residents of the growing city: the immigrants who were crowded into lower Manhattan, inhabiting the deplorable slums of the Lower East Side and the Bowery, and the middle class and affluent American-born "nativists"—those who believed that only those born here on United States soil had a right to any of the privileges of American citizenship.

The conflict between these two groups surfaced with violence in the streets on a number of occasions, but one polarizing event finally brought the simmering animosities to a head: the opening of two simultaneous productions of *Macbeth* in May 1849. One of these took place at the Astor Opera House in Manhattan, while the other performed at the Broadway Theater a few blocks away.

The Astor Opera House's *Macbeth* featured William Charles Macready, a famous English actor who enjoyed a prolonged, increasingly tense rivalry with his American counterpart, Edwin Forrest—at the time one of the most revered and popular actors in the country. The two actors had toured across the United States and through England, often performing the same plays as Forrest challenged Macready's prowess, allowing the crowds to decide which was the better actor. Not surprisingly, the American media preferred Forrest, while the English media lauded Macready.

After two such tours in each country, the rival actors agreed to star in *Macbeth* in New York, the crowning event of their remarkable tour. The people of New York City seemed to embrace the idea, while the big-city media filled pages with their analysis of the two famous actors. Edwin Forrest represented the interests of the immigrants: a man who grew up in the Bowery and gained fame and fortune through the sweat of his brow and his exemplary talent. Macready, meanwhile, represented everything the immigrant culture despised—aristocratic Anglo-Saxon background, wealth, and entitlement. The two actors may have been a perfect match of talent and skill onstage, but to the crowds who bought blocks of tickets to their performances, they could not have been more diametrically opposed. The lower classes set out to destroy Macready's ability to perform and send him back to England in shame.

When the production at Astor Opera House opened on May 7, 1849, the immigrant faction purchased hundreds of tickets in the balconies—not to enjoy the performance, but to make it impossible for it to go forward. They filled their pockets and bags with rotting vegetables and eggs, old shoes, and bottles of foul substances, and hurled these objects at the stage every time Macready appeared. The actors valiantly continued their performance, though they finally gave up trying to be heard over the catcalling and hissing, pantomiming the action for as long as they could stand the barrage of hatred that showered them. Meanwhile, just down the street, Edwin Forrest entertained a rapt audience who cheered every reference to Macbeth's takedown of the Anglo noblemen.

After such a miserable experience, it's no surprise that Macready called it quits and planned to depart for home on the next boat—but a coalition of wealthy New Yorkers convinced him to stay, and he took the stage as Macbeth again on May 10.

This time, the city's officials knew what to expect, and they prepared for the worst. Mayor Caleb S. Woodhull called out the state militia, stationing 350 men in Washington Square Park, 100 men outside the Astor Opera House, and another 150 men inside. Determined not to allow the wealthy nativists to ride roughshod over its citizens, the Tammany Hall political machine—the deeply corrupt but symbolic champion of the downtrodden immigrant society—mobilized its own street forces to gather at the opera house to embarrass the English descendants. They handed out tickets to Macready's show for free, attempting to fill the upper levels with working people, and crowded the streets with as many as ten thousand demonstrators. The working classes brought rocks to lob at the theater, grappling with the police and militia who fought to push them back.

When word went out that the people with free tickets had been screened out of the audience and turned away at the theater doors, a cadre attempted to set fire to the building. Rocks and stones flew, breaking windows and dislodging bricks in the opera house walls. Amid showers of glass shards and chunks of wall, the audience began to panic . . . but Macready and the rest of the cast continued the play, once again pantomiming the action until the last words of the last act, when the beleaguered actor donned a disguise and slipped out, never to return to New York.

Outside, bedlam replaced whatever order the police had dreamed they could maintain. The mayor finally called out the state regiment and they opened fire into the crowd at point-blank range. As many as 31 people died of gunshot wounds and 48 more were wounded, and another 141 were injured by rocks and debris flying through the air. Fifty to seventy policemen suffered injuries as well. The Astor Opera House attempted another season after this incident, but it did not survive the dramatic change in its reputation as a result of the riot, finally closing down after just a few performances.

Even beyond the violence, the lasting result of this event was its effect on the perception of Shakespeare's works in America for generations to come. Once considered popular entertainment, plays by English playwrights became the domain of highbrow audiences, moving uptown and away from the working classes. The immigrant cultures gravitated to burlesques, vaudeville, and musical entertainment that could be performed in smaller venues, not the grand opera houses and theaters of the upper classes. The divide between the wealthy and the not began with one play in two houses—and the curse of *Macbeth* became the catalyst for the great entertainment divide in popular culture.

Would such a demonstration have taken place if the two actors had performed *Hamlet* or *King Lear*? It seems likely, but we will never know for certain, and the Astor Place Riot certainly cemented this incident in the canon of the curse.

STILL CURSED TODAY

Macbeth as a concept may frighten many theater professionals, but it certainly hasn't affected the frequency with which theaters mount productions of it. With more productions come more stories of accidents, injuries, lawsuits, and sheer bad luck.

In 1988, a staggering number of problems followed a New York–born production of the Scottish Play as it lurched its way to Broadway. Starring Christopher Plummer in the title role, the production accumulated a downright wacky total of changes in artistic and production staff: three directors, six stage managers, two set designers, two lighting designers, five Macduffs, and six other cast changes. The cast also suffered a miserable twenty-six cases of the flu, and a range of wounds including torn and damaged ligaments and groin injuries. The venerable Plummer nursed a bad knee and a degenerating disk in his neck throughout the play's pre-Broadway tour, arriving at rehearsals in a wheelchair to allow his body to heal before evening performances. And such performances: The original director, Ken Frankel, had been fired and replaced by Stratford Shakespeare Festival director Robin Phillips, who had been ordered to transform the production. The valiant cast performed the Frankel production every evening and rehearsed the completely different Phillips production every day, a mind-bending task even for a cast of seasoned professionals.

The piece de resistance came when the old production finally ended and the cast transferred to the new production on a new set. Actor Thomas Schall tells the story in a podcast recorded by the Reduced Shakespeare Company, another New York City troupe.

Blocking changes, revised traffic patterns, and new prop assignments turned many of the scene changes into potential hazards—and with Plummer resting instead of rehearsing, it fell to the stage manager to fill him in on what had changed before the curtain rose for each evening's performance. Schall, who served as fight captain for the production as well as playing a character known only as First Murderer, was onstage for the tricky scene in which Banquo gets murdered on a darkened stage.

"So we go out and we do the murder of Banquo, and the light is struck out and it's dark," Schall said. "My blocking at that point is to exit through portal number one. My blocking [in the Ken Frankel production] used to be that I exit at portal number one, grab the candelabra, set it, turn around and exit again. What I didn't know is that every night, Plummer would follow me onstage as I set the candelabra."

Robin Phillips's new blocking did not require Schall to set the candelabra. Instead, the prop master set it—so when Plummer saw the candelabra go out onstage, he simply followed it . . . and never saw Schall coming at him.

"I smack into him in the dark," the still-chagrined Schall said, "and knock out his front tooth."

When the curtain fell at the end of the scene, Schall went out to Plummer to see if he was injured. "He says, 'Some asshole ran into me in the dark,'" Schall related. "I say, 'Oh, that asshole was me.'"

Schall fully expected to be fired before the night was out, but, happily, Plummer was not a petty man. "He was staggeringly gracious about it," Schall confirmed. "He went and chewed out the stage manager."

To be fair, what with transforming one play by day and managing the performances of another one by night, the stage manager probably hadn't slept in days, Schall noted.

Remarkably, the Scottish Play's casualty list continues to this day. As recently as 2013, a one-man reimagining of *Macbeth*, starring Alan Cumming and produced by the National Theatre of Scotland, enjoyed a limited run at Jazz at Lincoln Center in midtown Manhattan before moving on to Broadway. Stagehand Jason Makula, who was on the house crew for the production, enjoyed it considerably less, however—a piece of scenery crashed down on him during one of the performances, causing injuries severe enough for him to pursue a vigorous lawsuit against the National Theatre. After a year of wrangling, Makula won his suit to the tune of $2.37 million, claiming that the theater company had failed to use proper equipment to remove the stage wall, leaving it in "an unsafe, defective, hazardous and/or dangerous condition."

THE ANTIDOTE

So how can you ward off the curse if you are backstage rehearsing anything but the Scottish Play, and someone says the ill-fated general's name or quotes the play in your presence? One recommended remedy instructs you to leave the room, close the door, spin three times, and say a curse word of your choosing (the French are fond of *merde*, which means excrement). Others suggest that instead of the curse word, you quote one of Shakespeare's other plays: for example, Puck's epilogue from *A Midsummer Night's Dream*, Act V, Scene 2 ("If we shadows have offended . . ."), or a greeting from *The Merchant of Venice*, Act III, Scene 4 ("Fair thoughts and happy hours attend on you").

Once you've completed this short ritual, knock on the door and ask to be allowed back into the room you left. (As you must be given permission to reenter the room, this device provides a good way to punish a cast member who just can't stop quoting the cursed play.)

If you don't have the protective barrier of a door to close, quickly quote Act I, Scene 4 of *Hamlet*, another Shakespeare masterpiece—"Angels and ministers of grace defend us!"—and hope for the best.

4

THE CURSE OF
MAMIE O'ROURKE

East Side, West Side, all around the town
The tots sang, "Ring-a-rosie," "London Bridge is falling down."
Boys and girls together, me and Mamie O'Rourke,
We tripped the light fantastic on the sidewalks of New York.

—James W. Blake and Charles Lawlor, 1894

There was a time in the history of the Belmont Stakes, the last race in the coveted Triple Crown of thoroughbred horse racing, when the strains of "The Sidewalks of New York" bounced through the grandstand as the horses paraded to the gate. From 1956 until 1996, the swaying waltz written by Charles Lawlor, with its spritely, nostalgic lyrics by James W. Blake and Lawlor, served as the anthem to the Belmont's home city—just as "My Old Kentucky Home" honors the home state of the Kentucky Derby, and "Maryland, My Maryland" plays every year before the running of the Preakness at Pimlico Race Course in Baltimore.

In 1997, Belmont Park replaced the old standard with Frank Sinatra's seminal recording of the Fred Ebb and John Kander hit, "New York, New York," and horse-racing fans wish that the management of Belmont Park would jolly well bring "Sidewalks" back.

How could the simple replacement of a song create such an undercurrent of suspicion and distress? There seems to be a mysterious connection between the song and horses' ability to win the Triple Crown. Since Belmont Park stopped playing "Sidewalks," no horse with wins in the Kentucky Derby and Preakness has taken home the final jewel in the royal headpiece of thoroughbred racing.

This is not for lack of trying. The list of horses with a shot at the Triple Crown includes some of the finest steeds in racing: Silver Charm in 1997, Real Quiet in 1998, Charismatic in 1999, the auspiciously named War Emblem in 2002, Funny Cide in 2003, 2004's Smarty Jones, and Big Brown in 2008. In 2012, a horse named I'll Have Another seemed destined to win the Belmont, but was scratched before the race because of a leg injury. And 2014's entrant and two-race winner, California Chrome, looked ready to beat the curse, but was bested by a horse that had not even run in the Derby or the Preakness.

Ask any thoroughbred horse-racing fan, and they will tell you that the trouble started when Sinatra's song replaced "Sidewalks."

WHAT MAKES "SIDEWALKS" A LUCKY CHARM?

It's hard to pin down exactly why "The Sidewalks of New York" has risen to become the reason for the curse on the Belmont Stakes. The song, popular back in the 1890s—a time before every home had a radio or a phonograph—became a public favorite when singer Lottie Gilson sang it at Miner's Bowery Theatre in New York City in 1894. Demand for the sheet music led to more copies being sold of this song than any other song at that time, before composer Charles Lawlor sold his rights to the song, according to a *New York Times* interview with Lawlor in 1924. "I know the sales must have been up in the millions," Lawlor told the *Times* reporter. "How much did I get for that song? Why, just $5,000, and this I split fifty-fifty with my friend, James W. Blake . . . who was good at writing little squibs. He helped me put the words together."

Lawlor and Blake wrote the song together in August 1894 while standing in the haberdashery where Blake worked as a salesman. Lawlor, an Irish immigrant and vaudevillian who arrived in New York when he was seventeen years old, came up with the melody during an evening of controlled inebriation. He woke up in the middle of the night with the song and some of the lyrics running through his head, and enlisted his friend Blake's help in finishing it. The names sprinkled through the song came primarily from Blake, who used the actual names of friends and neighbors from his own childhood—including Mamie Rorke, who taught him to dance. Lucky for Mamie, her name rhymed conveniently with New York, gaining her a tiny piece of immortality by placing her in the song's chorus. Over the years and the song's many updates as it passed from one performer to the next—not the least of whom were Mel Tormé, Duke Ellington, and the Grateful Dead—Mamie's last name became "O'Rourke," giving greater emphasis to her Irish heritage.

Maintaining its popularity for thirty years through performances, sheet music passed down through generations, and early recordings, "The Sidewalks of New York" became synonymous with the turn-of-the-twentieth-century life of immigrant families in Manhattan and its surrounding boroughs. That's how it found its way to every ear in 1924, thirty years after its original publication, when presidential candidate and New York State Governor Alfred E. Smith adopted it as the theme song of his campaign.

The song did not act as a lucky charm for Al Smith, however. The Democratic Convention of 1924, held in New York City at Madison Square Garden, set records that had nothing to do with catchy theme songs. It took no less than 103 ballots for the delegates to nominate a presidential candidate, and the winner was not Al Smith. In a heated battle fueled by the active involvement of the Ku Klux Klan (causing this convention to earn the nickname "the Klanbake"), the delegates finally selected compromise candidate John W. Davis and his running mate, Charles W. Bryan of Nebraska. Don't worry if you haven't heard of these two; they were roundly defeated in the 1924 election by Calvin Coolidge, the sitting vice president of our twenty-ninth president, Warren G. Harding. Al Smith returned in 1928, won the Democratic nomination, and ran for president with "The Sidewalks of New York" as his theme song once again, but it served him no better. Smith lost the election to Herbert Hoover, and when he could not grab the nomination again in 1932 (losing it to Franklin Roosevelt), he finally stopped running for public office.

So Smith's choice of "Sidewalks" for his campaign song did not make him a winner—and it was not selected as the Belmont's iconic song because it carried some special good-luck magic. In fact, only three horses took the Triple Crown during the years that "Sidewalks of New York" played the horses to the post. Secretariat, roundly considered one of the greatest horses of all time, raced to the win in 1973. Just four years later, Seattle Slew won in 1977. The following year, the magnificent racehorse Affirmed won the Triple Crown.

FINDING THE RIGHT CURSE

In a sport as steeped in tradition as thoroughbred horse racing, any break with the tried and true gives spectators pause. Blaming a change that has nothing to do with the track, the horses, the jockeys, the owners, or anyone else involved with the race itself is exactly what sports fans do, whether they follow football, baseball, rugby, curling, America's Cup sailing, or thoroughbred racing.

In 2008, after Big Brown lost the Belmont, racing historian Bennett Liebman took a stab at explaining the then-thirty-year drought in Triple Crown winners. In a column in the *New York Times*, he examined the many theories involving curses on the Belmont.

Some believed that there was a specific curse on the 2008 race, Liebman noted, but "there was no smoking gun, no Bambino, not even a billy goat to make this curse credible." He then harkened back to 2004, when Smarty Jones had failed to bring home the third win, and this bad luck had been attributed to "a general curse against Philadelphia sports franchises and figures." Smarty Jones had appeared on the cover of *Sports Illustrated* before running the Belmont, extending the "traditional *Sports Illustrated* curse" to this horse.

Still Liebman searched for the right forces of evil that might be preventing a Triple Crown win at Belmont. "While my head tells me there is no curse, my heart tells me there is a curse," he continued. "It's the curse of the 'Sidewalks of New York.'" He affirmed that the fact that seven Crown-eligible horses have come to Belmont since 1997 and have been defeated coincides with the change in the theme song. "Maybe it's the revenge of Mamie O'Rourke," he postulated. "Perhaps she's tripping up the Triple Crown contenders on the sidewalks of Elmont. . . . If we care about tradition and the Triple Crown, it's time to restore the 'Sidewalks of New York' to its proper spot as the official song of the Belmont."

If the strength of a curse can be measured by the size of the crowd that embraces it, then the Curse of Mamie O'Rourke must be a powerful force indeed. Six years after Liebman's column, writers for the *New York Times*, *Atlantic*, and *Washington Post* all reconsidered the curse before California Chrome ran for the Triple Crown in 2014. So convincing was the case for the song that Belmont Park officials brought it back to the race on June 7, 2014, requesting that Sammy "the Bugler" Grossman play the song on his herald trumpet just before the race.

This resurrection apparently was not enough for Mamie, however. California Chrome lost the race to Tonalist, a horse that had not run in either the Kentucky Derby or the Preakness.

Perhaps Mamie is holding a grudge. In 2010, Belmont Park selected Jay-Z and Alicia Keys's "Empire State of Mind" as the theme song for the Belmont Stakes, looking to attract the interest of a younger audience and to update the race's image. The choice of song turned out to be a bad match for the traditional audience and the tone of the racing event, however, and "New York, New York" returned the following year. "Sidewalks" remained a distant afterthought.

THE REALITIES OF RACING

I had the opportunity to discuss the Curse of Mamie O'Rourke with Jenny Kellner, assistant director of communications for the New

York Racing Association. "The more people talk about the curse, the happier we are," she told me. "But there's no curse on the Belmont."

Horse racing has changed in the decades since the last Triple Crown winners, she explained. "Horses just don't race as often anymore. In the 1970s, when Seattle Slew and Secretariat won the Triple Crown, horses raced much more often. Affirmed ran nine times as a two-year-old, and he had four starts as a three-year-old before the Derby. Today, a horse may run only five or six times. They don't run as often or as far."

The winning horses of the 1970s also ran against a much smaller field of competitors, she noted. "Seattle Slew ran against eight other horses in the Belmont, and Secretariat ran against four. Affirmed ran against four in the Belmont. In 2014, California Chrome ran against ten horses! The field just keeps getting bigger and bigger, and it gets harder and harder to make it through."

Equally important, horses don't have to run in the Kentucky Derby and the Preakness to race in the Belmont. Many of the Triple Crown contenders now find themselves running against horses that are not spent from running two other major races in the last five weeks. With its six-figure purse for the winner, the Belmont is an attractive race for horses that can train exclusively to win it, rather than taking on the entire Triple Crown challenge. "Tonalist [the horse that beat California Chrome] was trained just for the Belmont," said Kellner. "He was coming off one really good prep race."

With all of these factors in play, however, it can't hurt to bring your superstitions to the track, she concluded. "We are very happy to have people come and whistle 'Sidewalks,'" she said.

THE MISSING PIECE

Rational explanations help us understand the world of horse racing, but not all questions can be answered by reasoned discourse. We still have one final query: Why would a young girl from the late 1800s want to curse a horse race in the twenty-first century?

The fact is that no one really knows. Mamie Rorke did not become a public figure whose motives might have specific, well-known targets. Perhaps her spirit is angry that her song no longer represents New York City at the Belmont Stakes, but returning the song to its accustomed place in 2014 did not defuse the curse.

David Hinckley of the *New York Daily News* took a stab at understanding Mamie in a story published in 2002. "Did she have dark hair? Red hair? Blue eyes? What did she wear to a sidewalk waltz on a summer evening?" he asked. "We are not even certain of her age. . . . She was most likely a teenager, old enough to waltz but young enough to still want to come out and play."

If you know something of the Irish immigration story in New York City, you know that many of the newly arriving immigrants of the 1850s through the 1870s were relegated to the worst part of the city, a Lower East Side area known as Five Points, where poverty, tenement living, and criminal activity made daily life very difficult for its residents. "We do know that Mamie O'Rourke very likely enjoyed a level of respectability not accorded to her mother or even older siblings, because the New York Irish of the mid-1890s were not the Irish of the 1850s," Hinckley went on. "For starters, they were no longer seen primarily as the criminal class. The percentage of violent crimes committed by the Irish had dipped from 60% in the 1850s to less than 10%—in part because they now had less need to commit crimes."

By Mamie's day, New York City had its first Irish mayor, William Grace, and programs to educate young Irish children had moved more than sixty thousand children off the streets and into schools, dramatically increasing literacy rates and future work opportunities. Mamie would have a working-class or even middle-class future ahead of her, a very different life from what her parents may have faced.

Why would such a young woman curse a horse race? It's an unanswerable question, but that won't stop racing fans from speculating that the spirit of a fiery Irish lass from beyond the grave might have undue influence over which horse crosses the finish line first on a summer afternoon in June in Elmont, New York.

Update: While this book was in production, the venerable horse American Pharoah—winner of both the Kentucky Derby and the Preakness—took an easy lead at the top of the Belmont Stakes on June 6, 2015, and galloped to a comfortable win in just over two minutes and twenty-six seconds. This remarkable horse took the Triple Crown and ended any talk of a curse on the race. "The Sidewalks of New York," which had returned in 2014 and failed to bring about a Triple Crown winner, was not heard before the 2015 race. Instead, Frank Sinatra sang the horses and riders into the gate. Perhaps Mamie O'Rourke felt that a horse as mighty as American Pharoah deserved the crown—or perhaps she had tired of the whole ordeal. Whatever the cause, the result made history.

5

THE LOST SOULS OF
SENECA COUNTY

If you've ever driven by Willard State Hospital—formerly Willard
Asylum for the Chronic Insane—in Ovid, New York, chances are
you felt a deep and urgent need to shudder. The very idea of an asylum operating in 1869, when Willard opened, brings up images of
techniques used before we had medications and modern therapies—
back when mental illnesses had names like "lunacy" and "hysteria,"
and those suffering from these illnesses were confined, restrained,
and isolated.

Let me relieve some of the inherent creepiness you may feel
about Willard: Patients here fared better than many mentally ill
individuals of the era, thanks to the insights of New York Surgeon
General Sylvester D. Willard, who saw the need to remove people
with mental illness from almshouses—institutions for the poor—and
place them in surroundings designed to deal humanely with their
specific issues. He secured 440 acres in the Finger Lakes for this purpose, and while he did not live to see the asylum he had ordered, the
medical center he imagined became the largest facility of its type in
the United States.

Those who have toured the remnants of the Willard facility since
its closing in 1995 learned about the methods used there to treat
the mentally ill. There were ice baths and electric shock treatments—
considered sound medicine for much of the twentieth century—but
as the fields of psychiatry and psychology grew, these therapies were
replaced by activities and medicines that had a more long-term positive effect. Willard strove to do the best for its patients, making it an

asylum in the truest sense of the word, and a place of solace for those who had been mistreated in facilities not equipped to handle their illnesses.

The first patient, Mary Rote, arrived in chains from the Columbia County poorhouse, where she had lived in squalor for decades with no clothing or bed, and no appropriate treatment for whatever dementia or other mental illness she had. Other arrivals had lost the use of their legs because they had been kept in irons or chains for years, and many came with records that informed Dr. John B. Chapin, medical superintendent of Willard, that the previous institution had tried everything to "cure" them—flogging, hanging the patient by his or her thumbs, even keeping one in a crate less than four feet square.

At Willard, arriving patients were treated with the first kindness they had experienced in years, or maybe ever. Workers dispensed with their chains and irons immediately, helped them bathe and provided clean clothing, and gave them full medical examinations. Patients lived in quarters with beds and all the appropriate necessities for comfort, ate hot meals, and were treated like human beings rather than the poor, rejected casualties of an intolerant society.

"The whole atmosphere of the place was one of peace, quiet and contentment," noted a report written by members of the State Charities Association of Erie County after their inspection in 1887. "The insane in the wards were clean, tidy, well-clothed, and quiet. Many of them were pleasantly occupied in bright, sunny sitting rooms, comfortably and appropriately furnished. They were reading, sewing or otherwise engaged. The bathrooms leading from the corridors had pretty tile floors and were perfectly free of unpleasant odors. The attendants were alert, attentive, on the look-out for their charges, and averaging one [attendant] for every eleven on the quiet wards and one to five for disturbed patients."

Just as important to their well being, many patients at Willard had the opportunity to work, providing them with skills and socialization as well as the therapeutic benefits of being busy and productive. Residents performed jobs in the gardens and the canning plant, made shoes, repaired mattresses, sewed clothing and bed linens, manufactured brooms and items from tin, polished floors in the wards, and baked bread. For patients who eventually left Willard, this activity gave them skills they could use in normal society.

If this place was such an improvement over conditions in poorhouses and workhouses across the state, why are so many of the souls who died here still haunting Willard Asylum?

GHOSTS THAT WALK BY NIGHT

Buildings that were part of the asylum have been repurposed in recent days, used by the New York State Department of Corrections and Community Supervision. Today the Willard Drug Treatment Center (WDTC), a specialized state prison for convicts with drug dependencies, operates a nine-hundred-bed, voluntary treatment center in some of the buildings used by the former mental asylum.

Staff members have spoken of a number of strange occurrences. Several report apparitions of people walking the halls, particularly a woman with long red hair. Doors open and close themselves when there are no people nearby. The screams of a woman alarm staff members in the middle of the night, but they find no one awake, in peril, or otherwise agitated.

"Two sergeant lieutenants said they saw something, heard a woman screaming at them," reported Melvin Williams, WDTC superintendent, on A&E's *Paranormal State* during the television show's first season. The episode aired on February 25, 2008. "They packed up and left the next day."

His story was repeated by another (unidentified) staff member on the Travel Channel's *Destination Fear.* "There were corrections officers here who spent the night," she said, "and in the middle of the night, there were men who got up, physically left the building, and just left their belongings, didn't want to come back to get them or anything else. They just left."

Williams himself added, "These were mainly security supervisors, so they have seen and handled a lot that most people don't have to handle. Yet there's definitely something here, whether you call it paranormal, otherworldly . . . something else is here."

Paranormal State brought in a psychic, a recording device that they said would capture and play back the voices of the dead, and even a demonologist to determine if the spirits were trapped in Willard's buildings by an evil force. They performed a ceremony to release them, and then declared them freed. Wasn't that easy?

If only it truly were so simple, said Jane Anderson of Port City Paranormal in Wilmington, North Carolina, who also brought a team to Ovid and investigated the ghost activity at Willard. "There is a lot of activity there," she said in a phone conversation with me. "We met several [spirit] personalities. One woman was so very friendly, and she asked us what we were doing. We heard a little girl ask, 'Can we come with you?'"

Anderson believes that the spirits at Willard are mostly staff members, though she and her team did encounter patients as well. "The patients seemed to be suffering," she said. "We were talking to one fellow, and we asked him where he was. He said, 'Paris.' If you know anything about psychiatry and the elderly, you know that people get confused. He may have thought he was in Paris because of the confusion he had when he died. You are in death what you were in life."

Spirits often remain in a place they enjoyed or felt comfortable during their lives, Anderson said. "There's also an association with guilt, unfinished business, or they miss a loved one. There are a lot of reasons for a spirit to remain here."

While Anderson defends strongly the good character of the people who wander the halls of Willard in spirit form, she can point to incidents in which one or more of the spirits attempted to harm her and her husband, fellow paranormal investigator Doug Anderson. "There was one nurse who actually walked through Doug at one point," she said. "He was breathless, disoriented. And I went through a door, and something was pushing the door closed on my fingers. This thing tried to harm me."

Later, a black mist close to the floor suddenly became animated, rose up, and covered Doug, choking him. "The mist then retreated to the top corner in the back of the room, out of our reach," she said. "They tried to hurt us because they misunderstood our intentions. These are human beings. If they feel threatened, they will lash out."

What makes these spirits so restless? As Anderson speculated, do they have unfinished business at Willard that keeps them from moving off into the afterlife in peace?

THE CURSE OF STATE LEGISLATION

The answer for this may lie, at least in part, in the state-enforced anonymity of Willard's patients—a law that makes it impossible to determine, or even to guess, who these souls actually may be.

In 1927, New York State legislators signed the Mental Hygiene Law, a complex and detailed set of statutes that calls for—among many other things—the complete confidentiality of a person being treated for mental illness. This right to privacy extends to sealing medical records relating to the treatment the patient may have received. In the case of Willard Asylum, confidentiality extends beyond the grave, even to recording which deceased patient is buried in each of the numbered graves in Willard's extensive cemetery.

Essentially, this law has made it impossible to reunite any information about these patients with the descendants of their families, or even to supply information to families about where a long-lost loved one was laid to rest. A total of 5,776 unmarked graves in this cemetery contain the bodies of those who died here, forever sheltered by anonymity despite the time that has passed since their interment.

While we can respect the original purpose of this law and its interest in protecting the patient from exposure as a person with mental illness—especially at a time when such illnesses were not well understood—it has since created a difficult situation for people trying to locate a lost relative, or to find his or her last resting place.

Perhaps this is the reason that some souls continue to wander the halls of Willard Asylum, long after its use as a home for the mentally ill came to an end in 1995.

WHEN THE CURSE DISRUPTS THE AFTERLIFE

Let's review, for a moment, the definition of a curse that we established in this book's introduction. A curse implies the intent to harm, most often as retribution for a past injury. For a curse to exist, there must be consequences—that is, someone, be they group or individual, must actually feel the power of the curse's influence on their lives.

Here is my own theory about the ghosts of Willard Asylum.

I believe these ghosts remain here not only because this was their final resting place but also because the law has made it impossible for them to reunite with their families. The sealing of their medical records, the complete anonymity that stripped them of identity even in death, and the separation from loved ones for decades or an entire lifetime have kept these souls wandering the halls, looking for a way home. They are, essentially, cursed to remain anonymous forever.

Many of these souls may have been locked away at Willard because of a wide range of symptoms we would consider quite normal today: a public display of emotion (the condition popularly known as "hysteria," especially in women), being the victim of sexual or domestic abuse, drunkenness, demonstrating an overt interest in sex, homosexuality, or an inability to communicate in English.

As Port City Paranormal describes them on its website, "Not all were insane, many patients were misdiagnosed, some were only mildly retarded, some suffering from post partum depression, but others were just the elderly, the poor, the unwanted, or the very bothersome."

The Willard campus is not open for public tours, so we must rely on the accounts of employees at the DTC to report whether they continue to hear, see, and sense things that would indicate continued spirit activity. If the crew from *Paranormal State* truly did release them, perhaps these souls are finding their way to the families that have long given up on seeing their loved one again.

If not, and the spirits continue to inhabit the former asylum, perhaps they will be freed by the grassroots efforts in the Ovid area to retrieve the names that match the numbered grave markers in the Willard cemetery. Maybe closure will not be so far off for these lost souls, the people protected by the state and abandoned by time.

6

THE BLACK DOG OF
THE GREAT LAKES

England has its Jenny Greenteeth, the Slavic nations have Rusalka, Japan believes in the Kappa, and Australia fears the Bunyip—so it seems that just about everywhere you go, your peaceful swim or sail in wide waters can end in an encounter with a monster that will pull you down into a watery grave.

To our knowledge, however, these European and Pacific specters are all fairy stories, most likely invented by parents looking to instill a healthy respect for deep water in their young children. They pale in comparison to the Great Lakes' own malevolent spirit, one that has its origin in a most unlikely, very real creature.

I write, of course, of the Black Dog of the Great Lakes, a canine known to captains who have had the misfortune of meeting the great beast face to face—and whose story has been passed down by the handful of sailors and their commanders who have lived to tell the tale.

This gentle spirit was of the Canadian-bred Newfoundland breed, one of the sweetest tempered and friendliest canine varieties in the entire Westminster Kennel Club catalog. Naturally equipped with strong swimming ability, the enormous Newfoundland—weighing in at some 150 pounds—has been known to leap from the deck of a ship into the water to perform heroic rescues or to save its master from perils at sea. One of these massive animals even received credit for rescuing Napoleon Bonaparte when the general missed his footing while leaving his ship near Elba and plunged into the Mediterranean Sea.

Such a dog would never become an omen of certain death—at least, not of its own volition. Herein lies the tale of the Black Dog of the Great Lakes, an animal so wronged that it now prowls the lakes during inclement weather, looking for its revenge on the sailors who sent it to an undeserved and undignified end.

HOW A FRIEND BECAME A THREAT

The dog that now signals disaster on America's largest freshwater lakes began its life as a mascot, devoted to the sailors aboard its vessel. The name of the ship has been lost to history, but the deeds of the sailors will live on—for when they repaid their dog's loyalty with ridicule and death, the dark canine turned against man and ship, sending them to the depths of the largest lakes in North America.

Legend tells us that the dog's ship was sailing the Welland Canal up in Ontario, Canada, the manmade waterway that connects Lake Ontario with Lake Erie. The canal crosses the Niagara Peninsula, beginning with Port Weller and leading to Port Colborne, allowing ships to move around the impassable Niagara Falls. We don't know exactly which of the canal's eight locks the black dog's ship may have approached when the despicable incident occurred, but those who know the tale believe that the ship must have been close to the end of the flight of locks, because the sailors had become especially bored.

I must say a word of caution here to readers who are very fond of pets: The story I am about to tell you may be difficult to read, because it involves a level of cruelty of which you and I certainly are not capable. In fact, it's hard to imagine why these surly sailors decided to entertain themselves by hurting their devoted friend, even given the context of merchant ships in the mid-nineteenth century, when our current standards for decent and ethical treatment of animals were not so prevalent as they are today.

If you have continued to read, then here is the tale. Some who tell the story say that the sailors dropped the Newfoundland over the side of the ship to watch him swim, while others suggest that the dog fell off the boat of his own accord. Whichever is true, the black dog found itself in the water and began to swim alongside the ship, clearly expecting that his friends aboard would find a way to pull him up.

The sailors, however, did nothing at all to help the dog reboard the ship. Instead, they tormented the dog, taunting and laughing at him while he scratched for a foothold against the side. The Newfoundland, exhausted by the struggle, finally had no choice but to give up. He sank back into the water and breathed his last, his eyes on his former friends with a gaze that undeniably expressed the depth of their betrayal.

Whether the sailors felt remorse will never be known, but when the lock gate came down to seal the canal's waters into the chamber and lift the boat to the next level, the dog's corpse got stuck between the gate and the bottom of the canal. The lock could not close, so the water could not flow in and fill the chamber. The sailors found their ship trapped in place by their own folly.

With a schedule to keep and other ships behind them waiting for passage through the lock, the sailors had to act quickly—but they could not. For hours they worked to pull the dog's body out from under the gate, using whatever tools they could cobble together from the chains and rope they had onboard. You may hope that these cruel men were stuck there until their last day on earth, but they did manage to pull the dog's body free after several hours of effort, continuing on their way with at least a shade more regret than they may have felt when they allowed their mascot to perish.

A CENTURY OF CURSED SHIPS

Was this the end of the black dog's revenge? Our Newfoundland hero had only begun to exact the vengeance he deserved after his soggy death. Soon rumors and retellings spread about the sudden arrival of a large, black phantom dog on the deck of a merchant ship, an apparition that would materialize on one side of the ship, dash across the deck, and leap into the dark water below. The vision signaled a violent end, an impending shipwreck that would come in short order.

Some captains and crew lived to warn others of the black dog, somehow managing to stay alive in the frigid lake waters long enough to be rescued. Others were never heard from again, so we can only speculate about whether the black dog made himself known before the ships ran into trouble.

We don't know exactly when the black dog drowned and became the specter of destruction, so it's hard to guess exactly how many shipwrecks might have involved the dark animal's ghostly presence. We do know that once the Erie and Welland canals opened in the 1820s, shipping on the Great Lakes became the most important means of transporting goods from the New England and Mid-Atlantic states to the developing west. Nearly two thousand ships crossed each Great Lake with regularity, creating a significant amount of traffic in every direction and in every navigable season. When shipping companies pushed their spring and fall transportation seasons into the North Country winter, ships could be caught in storms that tore apart their hulls and dragged them down into the deep.

Literally thousands of ships sank in the waters of the Great Lakes, littering the bottoms of the lakes with their hulls and cargo. In Lakes Erie and Ontario, the two lakes that have shorelines in New York State, hundreds of ships met their doom. How many crewmembers may have seen the black dog before their ships were destroyed can never be known, but a few who survived speak of the dog, and of their attempts to heed the animal's warning.

The most vivid of these stories comes from the *Isaac G. Jenkins,* a schooner carrying wheat from Milwaukee to the port at Oswego, New York. According to an account retold by C. H. J. Snider in the article "Moonlight on the Lake," the ship was sailing quietly down Lake Erie on a peaceful night when the helmsman, the only person awake on the vessel, let out a yell that awoke every man aboard. "The

Black Dog!" he cried to anyone who would listen. "It came up over the weather rail in the moonlight!"

The helmsman claimed he saw the completely dry animal walk across the deck and over the lee rail, entering the water without so much as a ripple and vanishing into the night. As he told the story, the animal became larger in his recollection, with eyes of fire and its tongue lolling from its jaws.

When the ship reached dock in Chicago, the helmsman told the story again and again in a bar filled with Canadian sailors. By the time he returned to the ship, the helmsman had so worked up his fear that he begged the captain and crew to abandon the ship and save their own lives.

Captain John Brown's response was to give the helmsman a good swift kick, toss his gear onto the dock, and order the man off his ship for good. Yet the helmsman reappeared when the ship pulled into Port Robinson, once again imploring the captain to leave the ship. The captain responded with an equal level of violent language, but the helmsman would not give in. He continued to meet the ship at every lock as it passed through the Welland Canal, wailing that the crew and the ship were doomed. By this time the crew had become agitated as well, so when the *Jenkins* finally passed through the last lock and reached Port Dalhousie, Captain Brown set sail before he lost his crew in a mutiny of terror. Perhaps, in his own distraction, he did not notice that the other ships that had accompanied the *Jenkins* through the locks did not move ahead, as their captains decided to wait out the gale they had sighted.

That was on November 30, 1875. In the dark of that Lake Ontario night, the *Isaac G. Jenkins* foundered in the gale several miles north of Oswego, sinking with all eight of her crewmembers and two passengers on board.

"There was, however, one survivor of the *Isaac G. Jenkins*," reports author Terry Boyle in the book *Haunted Ontario 3: Ghostly Historic Sites, Inns, and Miracles.* "A short time later, a farmer sighted a dog coming ashore at Sheldon's Pond some miles up the westward of Oswego." The dog "dragged his hind legs as though paralyzed."

AN OMEN, NOT A KILLER

As the black dog has never been reported to harm anyone himself, there is another possible interpretation of his appearance on the deck of a ship just before it runs into trouble. Perhaps the still-loyal animal, attempting to bond with a new crew even in death, arrives to warn the sailors of the danger ahead.

Chambers Dictionary of the Unexplained tells us, "The appearance of a Black Dog is often interpreted as an omen of impending death or disaster for the person witnessing it—although in some areas, such as Essex [England], they traditionally have a protective function."

It's possible that sailors should take warning from the friendly canine, rather than viewing him with fear and panic. It could be that the Newfoundland simply wants the crew to batten down the hatches, look ahead for the obstacles or storms on the horizon, and navigate themselves away from the tragedy waiting to befall them.

If you regularly sail the Great Lakes, try telling this to your crew as the phantom black dog springs up onto your deck, crosses from port to starboard, and vanishes into the waves. Then check the second hand on your watch and see how long it takes your crew to demand that you head for the safety of the shore.

7

THE RANGERS, THE STANLEY CUP, AND THE CURSE OF 1940

By all accounts, the Madison Square Garden (MSG) Corporation had a spectacular year in 1940. Its home hockey team, the New York Rangers, won the National Hockey League championship and brought home the Stanley Cup, professional hockey's most coveted prize. The Garden also hosted professional boxing, circuses, and a number of other high-profile events, packing spectators into its eighteen thousand seats. The popularity of the Garden led to significant profits—enough to allow the corporation to pay off the mortgage on this relatively new arena, constructed in 1925 and the third to bear the Madison Square name.

We can imagine the jubilation the MSG Corporation's members must have felt. Paying off a massive mortgage right after a major win in an international sports competition would make anyone a bit cocky, even a little imprudent. Perhaps we could forgive them, then, for the way they celebrated this triumph. Perhaps we even could expect Saint Sebastian, whom Catholics consider the patron saint of athletics, to watch over them and mitigate the effects of their hubris.

What was the sinful act of desecration these bureaucrats committed? General John Reed Kilpatrick, president of the New York Rangers, led the Madison Square Garden Corporation's members in burning MSG's paid-off mortgage . . . in the bowl of the Stanley Cup.

This may seem a fairly innocuous deed to people who are not hockey fans, so let's take a moment for a quick history of the cup to help you keep up with the story.

There's only one Stanley Cup, passed from one championship team to the next each year, and the names of all the winning teams' players and management are engraved on wide metal bands stacked beneath the actual bowl of the cup. This gives the trophy a somewhat bulky and unwieldy appearance, but to those who receive it, it represents a towering history of champion-level play. Each of the bands around the base can be engraved with the rosters of thirteen winning teams, so the cup stands as a monument not only to the current year's champions but also to all the champions who have come before them.

With so much real and symbolic stature, the Stanley Cup takes on a reverential, almost sacred quality among tens of millions of fans throughout the United States and Canada. Imagine their ire, then, when the MSG Corporation desecrated their icon by burning a financial document in its bowl. Granted, this took place in 1940, long before television could bring footage of the flames into every home, but word spread the old-fashioned way: through hearsay, rumor, and the occasional newspaper story.

As the Rangers faced one losing season after another through the 1940s, the tale of the mortgage burning grew in significance and became part of the team's lasting lore. In the team's first fourteen years in existence, the Rangers won four Stanley Cup championships—the first in the 1926–1927 season, their inaugural season of play, and again in 1927–1928, 1932–1933, and 1939–1940. After the desecration of the Stanley Cup, however, their winning seasons ended. The curse had taken hold.

THE DUTTON DOUBLE WHAMMY

As if the curse of the Stanley Cup were not enough to seal the Rangers' fate, another incident involving Madison Square Garden management piled a second layer onto the original misfortune.

In the early days of the National Hockey League, New York City had a second major league team: the New York Americans. (Remarkably, these Americans are not related to the Rochester Americans upstate, which play in the American Hockey League.) This New York team played in Madison Square Garden from its opening in 1925, a fact that might make casual readers believe that the "Amerks" had more claim to MSG residency than the Rangers did. That's not how the league saw it, however; the Rangers frequently won championships, while the Amerks barely made it into the playoffs and never won a title game.

The Amerks' coach and general manager was well known to hockey fans: Norman Alexander Mervyn Dutton, better known as "Red"–a Western Canada Hockey League All-Star and a former Amerks player who eventually became president of the NHL. He became the coach at the request of the NHL while still playing for the team in 1935–1936, and stepped down as a player the following year to devote his time to team management. Red Dutton's easily sparked temper gained him a reputation as a firebrand, but this did nothing to harm his popularity.

In the 1937–1938 season, Amerks owner Bill Dwyer–a convicted bootlegger–found himself struggling to support the team when Prohibition ended, with legal and IRS issues sapping his ill-gotten wealth. The NHL interceded in 1937 and forced Dwyer out, taking ownership of the team and giving Dutton a fairly free hand in managing it. Dutton rewarded them with the third winning season in Amerks' history, finishing with a 19-18-11 record–but they lost to the Chicago Black Hawks in the semi-finals, ending the season without a shot at a championship.

Twice more the Amerks took a run at the playoffs, and twice more were they defeated before they could approach a Stanley Cup win. As if their luck could not get worse, a new obstacle to success arrived in the 1941–1942 season: World War II took away many of the Amerks' players, as they were drafted or enlisted in the military and got shipped overseas. Seeing the obvious about a team fractured into bits, Dutton suspended team play until the war was over.

In 1943, the NHL asked Dutton to become its president. He agreed on one condition: the NHL had to commit to reinstating the New York Amerks when the war ended and the players returned from the military. The NHL agreed, but when the time came in 1946 to put the Amerks back on the ice, the league reneged on their promise—even though Dutton had arranged for $7 million in financing to build his team a new arena. The true meaning was clear, as far as Dutton was concerned: the NHL as owner—and Madison Square Garden as host, even though a new arena would become the Americans' home—preferred the more successful New York Rangers over the struggling Amerks. Dutton's famous temper took over, and he informed the assembly, "You can stick your franchise up your ass."

History reports that Dutton later declared that the Rangers would never win another championship as long as he was alive.

I say that "history" reports this, because there are no journalistic accounts of this outburst in any of the important newspapers of the day. Whether this took place in a closed-door meeting with select NHL officials or in a tavern among friends, the moment itself did not become a matter of public record—and nearly a decade of losing seasons passed before the fans began to consider that something more than bad luck might be up with the New York Rangers.

A FIFTY-FOUR-YEAR DROUGHT

If you visit the New York Rangers website at rangers.nhl.com and scroll through the Rangers History pages, you won't find a single mention of Dutton's Curse or the Curse of 1940. You will, however, read accounts of one close call after another as the Rangers fought to win another Stanley Cup in the shadow of their early success.

In the years after the Amerks' dissolution, the National Hockey League entered a period known as the Original Six Era, when just six teams competed for the Stanley Cup from the 1942–1943 season all the way to the playoffs in 1967. Throughout the 1940s and 1950s, the Rangers reached the Stanley Cup playoffs only once, in 1950. In the 1960s and 1970s, the team experienced a renaissance of sorts, reaching the playoffs nine consecutive times . . . but still not turning the tide in their favor. Their closest brush with the Stanley Cup came in 1971–1972, when they lost a six-game playoff series to the Boston Bruins, led by Canadian defenseman Bobby Orr—a player whose name is famous even to those of us who are not lifelong hockey fans.

After this narrow defeat, the Rangers learned that New York was about to gain another hockey team: the New York Islanders, named for their Long Island home in Nassau County and soon to become worthy rivals for the Cup. The Islanders rose to win the conference championship in 1978–1979, and they took the Stanley Cup in four consecutive seasons from 1979–1980 to 1982–1983, effectively shutting out the Rangers and deepening the belief in the selection of curses that haunted the beleaguered New York City team.

Continuing to come close to the finals in one tournament after another for the next decade, the Rangers barreled into the 1990s with a strong team and high hopes that they would finally see the end of their long run without a championship. We can't help but wonder if a murmur of anticipation went through the locker room in March 1987 when Red Dutton passed away at eighty-nine years of age. Perhaps, finally, the then-forty-seven-year losing streak would abate, and the Rangers would find their way to the big win they had sought for so long.

Whether a lingering shroud of ill will continued to lie over the team for another several years, or the rest of the NHL league simply had stronger squads, the Rangers still could not net themselves a win. In the 1991–1992 season, they scored a Presidents' Trophy, finishing the season with the best record in the league during the regular season . . . but they dodged success once again in the playoffs as the Pittsburgh Penguins pushed through to victory. When a series of injuries and losses landed the Rangers at the bottom of the league in the 1992–1993 season, team leadership knew that something dramatic would have to happen in 1993–1994 if they were to keep their fan base.

Picking up center Mark Messier—formerly of the winning Edmonton Oilers—and under the leadership of Mike Keenan, the Rangers pulled together in 1993–1994 with a strength their fans had not seen since 1940. They took the Presidents' Trophy with 52 wins and only 24 losses for the season, with a franchise record of 112 points, and defeated the New York Islanders in the playoffs with a winning sweep. The hotly contested Conference Finals series against the New Jersey Devils looked at first as if it would lead to the Rangers' fifty-fifth consecutive loss . . . but in the seventh game on their home ice at Madison Square Garden, a final goal scored in double overtime put New York's team over the top.

The Stanley Cup series pitted the Rangers against the Vancouver Canucks, a tough rivalry that pushed the playoff to seven games, once again bringing the Rangers home to MSG for the final round. The Rangers took an early 2–0 lead and Messier scored a third goal, and the Canucks could not keep up. The game ended with a 3–2 lead by the Rangers and the shattering, at last, of the five-decade curse.

The Rangers have gone on to take a division championship in 2011–2012 and 2014–2015, the conference championship in 2013–2014, and the Presidents' Trophy in 2014–2015, but there hasn't been another year like 1993–1994. The team has made the playoffs in seven of the last eight seasons as of this writing, so perhaps they are building to another big win—and so far, there's no talk of a new curse to prevent it.

8

THE DEATH OF A
PRESIDENT AND
THE TEAMS THAT
FAIL TO THRIVE

The 1901 Pan-American Exposition in Buffalo, New York, must
have been the grandest event ever produced in the United States
up to that time. Extending along the western edge of what is now
Delaware Park, this World's Fair covered 350 acres and literally lit
up the city, using power generated by Niagara Falls—twenty miles
away—to illuminate the entire exposition.

"Each evening, hundreds of thousands of eight-watt light bulbs
were gradually illuminated and outlined the buildings, reflecting
pools, fountains and sculptures that occupied the grounds," the Theodore Roosevelt Inaugural National Historic Site website tells us
about the exposition. "This was the first massive display of electric
power to take place in the United States. . . . In the eyes of people
accustomed to gas, oil, and candlelight, the effect was both beautiful
and startling."

Eight million people attended the extraordinary event, coming
to Buffalo from across the continent beginning May 1, 1901, and
continuing through November 2. The city received $500,000 from the
federal government to construct dozens of temporary buildings on
the site, each showcasing a different aspect of modern life. Brightly

colored and festive, the exposition's ersatz town gained the nickname "Rainbow City," and its mix of classical and Spanish architecture gave a politically important nod to the fact that America included Central and South American countries as well as the English-speaking northern ones.

In one of these buildings—the Temple of Music—on September 6, 1901, US President William McKinley attended a public reception in the afternoon. President McKinley enjoyed meeting his public face to face, so he shook hands with hundreds of people as they moved through the building. When a young man with a bandaged right hand approached him just after 4 p.m., McKinley immediately offered his left hand to shake. He did not see the gun concealed in the man's hand under the bandage.

Leon Czolgosz fired two shots at point-blank range. Before he could fire a third shot, he was knocked to the ground by a waiter at the reception and quickly taken into police custody, and McKinley was rushed to the small first-aid hospital on the exposition grounds. There doctors removed one of the bullets from his body, but they could not locate the other—and, ironically, they had to work by gaslight, as the hospital had not been equipped with the brighter electric lights that festooned the outsides of all the buildings. The medical team closed the wound, but the remaining bullet did the job Czolgosz intended. Eight days later, on September 14, McKinley died of gangrene caused by the bullet left in his body.

That's the day, according to many present-day Buffalonians—especially its sports fans—that the city's luck began to go sour. Before the sun set that day, Vice President Theodore Roosevelt was sworn in as president of the United States at the home of Ansley Wilcox, 641 Delaware Avenue, where the National Park Service now manages a National Historic Site. But by the time Roosevelt took the oath of office, the die had been cast for Buffalo. The city's residents could look forward to more than a century of bad luck . . . particularly for its sports teams.

Wait. What?

THE "BUFFALO CURSE"

It started as a joke among fans of the National Football League's Buffalo Bills and the Buffalo Sabres, the city's National Hockey League team, but the worse the teams performed each season and the more close races to the championship they lost, the more seriously the fans viewed the curse.

We talked about the Bills in chapter 1 of this book, offering another paranormal explanation for their long losing streak. Buffalo's football team has not won a championship game since 1965, back when they were part of the American Football League and two years before there was a Super Bowl. The AFL merged with the NFL in 1970, and the Bills looked like they had a shot at the big show when they drafted O. J. Simpson, still one of the greatest running backs of all time. Simpson tallied up a long list of injuries along with his records, however, and Bills management traded him to the San Francisco 49ers in 1978.

More than a decade later, led by Coach Marv Levy, the Bills made it to one step away from greatness in four consecutive years. They played in the Super Bowl in 1990, 1991, 1992, and 1993 . . . and lost all four games. The team hasn't seen a playoff win since.

If the Bills' record seems dismal, the Buffalo Sabres' history of championship misses and achingly close losses would cause any die-hard fan to think carefully about forces beyond the team's control. Never a Stanley Cup winner and only once bringing home the Presidents' Trophy for the NHL's highest-scoring team, the Sabres have won three conference championships and six division championships as of this writing, making their eventual losses in the league championship series just that much more incomprehensible to the fans.

The BuffaloCurse.com website names the dissolution of the city's National Basketball Association team, the Buffalo Braves, as more proof of the curse on Buffalo sports—and it even suggests that the staggeringly long losing career of the Cleveland Browns football team may be connected to the McKinley assassination as well. The slain president had been the governor of Ohio, making many visits to Cleveland; Leon Czolgosz actually worked in Cleveland before moving to Buffalo. McKinley was born in the nearby town of Niles, further strengthening his connection to the Ohio city on Lake Erie—a lake it shares with Buffalo.

THE McKINLEY FACTOR

While there's no question that the professional major league sports teams in Buffalo (and Cleveland) have had far more than their fair share of bad luck, is it possible that President McKinley would specifically target pro sports with a curse?

In McKinley's day, Major League Baseball held sway as the national pastime, a sport in which Buffalo has never had a professional entry. Could the ill-fated president have conceived of a country with so many sports franchises, billions of dollars changing hands, players receiving million-dollar contracts, and more money than he would make in a lifetime spent on one advertisement on the Super Bowl broadcast? Even more to the point, could he have imagined fans so loyal that they would follow losing teams for generations?

The carefully anonymous creator of BuffaloCurse.com suggests that McKinley may have had an edge. It turns out that the president was a member of the "secret" society of Freemasons, a fraternal order known for its tradition of using symbolism, handshakes, and a number of other seemingly covert means of communication to identify one another across chapters and continents. The BuffaloCurse.com promoter suggests that this society is known to be evil, and that McKinley may have banded with his mason brothers to poison Buffalo's pastimes for many generations.

It's a fascinating theory, but there's a central problem with it: The Freemasons are not secret, and they are not evil. Masonic lodges and temples stand in just about every major city in America, as well as in metropolitan centers around the world, advertising the meeting places of this band of brothers (and sisters, more recently) for the world to see. While the symbols inscribed on these buildings can be puzzling, their meanings have been published in countless books and on many websites. The Freemasons are well known for their charitable works, their spiritual goals (many orders require their members to state their belief in a supreme being, and some will only accept practicing Christians), and the community leaders they attract and produce. There's not much evidence that the Freemasons regularly perpetrate curses on their members' enemies, even when a member has been wronged as violently as President William McKinley was in Buffalo.

BuffaloCurse.com states on its home page that its theories are meant as satire, so there's no need to put these concepts through the shredder. Suffice it to say that if McKinley cast a curse on Buffalo, he probably did so on his own, perhaps from a more powerful and paranormally flexible afterlife.

A CURSE-NADO

Or, perhaps, is there a conglomeration of curses coming together—a Curse-Nado, if you will—to keep any Buffalo team from reaching and winning a final championship?

In a fine discussion on Bleacherreport.com in November 2014, NFL analyst Gary Davenport suggested that some particularly bad luck for Buffalo that year, including the heaviest snowstorm ever recorded in the contiguous forty-eight states, could have been the result of a curse perpetrated more than a decade earlier by jilted Bills quarterback Doug Flutie.

In 1999, Flutie found himself inexplicably benched after leading the Bills to a 10–5 season record as they approached the playoff games. Head Coach Wade Phillips made the decision to take Flutie out of play, a move one ranking organization—Cold, Hard Football Facts—named "the worst head coaching decision in the 94-year history of pro football." Flutie and Phillips both watched from the sidelines as the Bills became victims of a play that is still known as "The Music City Miracle": With Buffalo leading 16–15 and only sixteen seconds left on the clock, Buffalo kicked a field goal that fell short, right into the hands of Lorenzo Neal of the Tennessee Titans. Neal threw a lateral pass to Kevin Dyson, who ran the ball all the way down to the Buffalo end zone for a winning touchdown. The Titans won the game 22–16 and went on to the Super Bowl (where they lost to the St. Louis Rams).

Flutie only remained with the Bills for one more season, but the effects of the now hashtag-immortalized #curseofflutie continue to be felt to this day—in fact, it followed Wade Phillips from team to team, jinxing the San Diego Chargers and even the powerhouse Dallas Cowboys in the years when Phillips became their head coach.

Are you keeping count? We're up to three curses so far: McKinley, Indian burial grounds (see chapter 1), and Flutie. There are more.

In 2000, the Bills brought a new face to the field: a big, blue, plushy, person-sized buffalo named Billy, the team's first costumed mascot since the 1980s. Billy has made a name for himself with his on-field antics, his ability to run a forty-yard dash, and an eyebrow-raising feat immortalized in a GIF: at a boys vs. mascots Pee Wee Football game, Bill vaulted over the entire Pee Wee offensive line in a move reminiscent of Troy Polamalu of the Pittsburgh Steelers.

Despite his apparent popularity, however, Billy Buffalo has irked sports writer Mike Sullivan. In a post on the football comedy site The Kick Is Good, Sullivan went so far in 2014 as to name Billy "a 7 foot bad luck charm." He continues, "The Buffalo Bills have not made the playoffs since Billy Buffalo was introduced. Coincidence? I think not."

Sullivan goes on to cite a long list of statistics that make his case, the most poignant of which include these:

14 Seasons Before Billy Buffalo	14 Seasons After Billy Buffalo
Winning Percentage: .605	Winning Percentage: .344
Regular Season Wins: 135	Regular Season Wins: 77
Playoff Appearances: 10	Playoff Appearances: 0
Super Bowl Appearances: 4	Super Bowl Appearances: *Please*

If you're willing to consider coincidences as causal relationships, the statistics in this table also apply exactly to the period since the Bills moved their training camp to St. John Fisher College in Pittsford, a suburb of Rochester, about sixty miles northeast of Buffalo. While I have searched for reasons that this move would act as a curse, none have come to the surface—and most who bring up this Rochester location cite the positive side: the opportunity to stop at Nick Tahou's in Rochester and order the establishment's famous "garbage plate," a gastric concoction of potatoes, baked beans, hot dogs, macaroni salad, onions, mustard, and spicy meat sauce. The Fisher curse has not caught on as a serious contender for Buffalo's woes, but it could be one more breath of wind in the already churning Curse-Nado.

SO, IS BUFFALO CURSED?

With fans as dedicated to the sinking ship that has been Buffalo professional sports, it's easy to understand why these long-suffering devotees would search for a supernatural reason for the teams' troubles.

It is not for me to second-guess the teams' management, players, strategy, or any other aspect of their long, long losing streaks. That being said, a groundswell of support has gone to the theory that something outside of these sports franchises—something mere mortals cannot understand—may be at work to prevent the Bills and the Sabres from becoming the winning teams their fans crave.

Only sheer determination will break the curse, just as it did for the New York Rangers in 1994 and the Boston Red Sox in 2004. These teams and others have shown that a powerhouse season can still take a team to the top of the league—and when they get there, the fans will be right there with them, face paint and official jerseys in place, to cheer them to the winning point at long last.

9

GUSTAV MAHLER AND THE CURSE OF THE NINTH SYMPHONY

It seems that the Ninth is a limit. He who wants to go beyond it must pass away. It seems as if something might be imparted to us in the Tenth which we ought not yet to know, for which we are not ready. Those who have written a Ninth stood too close to the hereafter.

—Arnold Schoenberg

Of all the conductors who have led the New York Philharmonic Orchestra and the Metropolitan Opera, only a handful have achieved the level of compositional immortality seized by Gustav Mahler.

A composer who believed that every one of his compositions should have the majesty and power of Ludwig van Beethoven's Ninth Symphony—one of the best known and most praised works in classical music—Mahler wrote works for full orchestras, incorporating operatic soloists and choruses along with the complete range of orchestral instruments. His unusual composing style made him a bridge between the classical music tradition of the nineteenth century and the new, modern sound of the early twentieth—paving the way for exciting composers including Dmitri Shostakovich and Benjamin Britten.

As Mahler established himself in New York City in 1908 as the principal conductor at the Met, he had more than one goal in mind.

Certainly musical excellence dominated his approach to his responsibilities at the opera, but he also knew that he would compose a new piece in the summer of 1908 after the current Met season . . . and this piece would be the dreaded ninth symphony, a work that he believed could be the kiss of death.

Not many composers have turned out enough work to reach a ninth symphony, but a number of Mahler's greatest influences did so—and did not live to see a tenth. Beethoven died in 1827 at age fifty-six, after completing Symphony No. 9. Franz Schubert died at thirty-one years old in 1828, sometime around the writing of his ninth (though renumbering of his symphonies after his death places his total at ten). Anton Bruckner, who did not quite complete his Symphony No. 9 in D Minor because of his failing health, died in 1896 at seventy-two. Antonin Dvorak, a contemporary of Mahler's, died after completing his ninth and most famous symphony, "The New World." All of these venerable composers influenced Mahler's work, and the fact that they all departed this world during or just after the completion of their ninth symphony aroused a superstition in him that he could very well be next.

If you're a fan of classical music, you may know that Wolfgang Amadeus Mozart wrote 41 symphonies, and Joseph Haydn wrote 104 symphonies. However, both of these brilliant composers wrote their symphonic works in a period before the symphony became the massive undertaking it is considered now. The turning point, many audiophiles would say, came with Beethoven, who elevated the art form to a new level of complexity that launched the Romantic era in orchestral music. When Beethoven died after completing his ninth symphony, superstitious music lovers believed his death set a precedent that influenced the fate of other major composers of that genre.

Mahler believed the die was cast, and his ninth symphony would be his last. In 1908, with his eighth symphony completed and the urge to continue to write still a driving force within him, he had reason to believe that his days were numbered.

"The year 1908 was traumatic for Mahler," wrote music journalist Peter Lefevre on the Chicago Symphony Orchestra website, "and intimations of mortality surrounded him while writing. . . . He'd lost his position as director of the Vienna Opera, had been diagnosed with endocarditis and was grieving the death of his 4-year-old daughter," who had perished from scarlet fever and diphtheria a year earlier.

The diagnosis of Mahler's congenital heart condition came within a month of the loss of his daughter, when the composer was just forty-seven years old. While he insisted in letters to his wife, Alma, that he would be able to live a full life, the realities and harbingers of death around him made him think carefully about the symphony he was about to write. He determined a course that he hoped would help him dodge the fate he saw on the horizon—essentially, cheating death by fooling it with words.

Making his living as a conductor, Mahler cherished his summers and the time they gave him to work uninterrupted in one of his studios in his native Austria. In the summer of 1908, he settled into a studio near the evergreen forests of Tyrol and began a symphonic work that would never receive a number. He titled the now-famous composition *Das Lied von der Erde*, or "The Song of the Earth."

The masterful work sprang from a text based on ancient Chinese poems, presenting six songs for two singers—notably a tenor and an alto (or a baritone if no alto was at hand), a fairly unusual combination for an entire song cycle. Mahler drew upon his experience in using voices in four of his previous symphonies, and he took the translations of the Asian poems from a text by Hans Bethge, who in turn had used translations by other German-language writers.

Mahler's frame of mind comes through poignantly in the poems he chose to set to music. Here's a sample from the first of the songs, "Das Trinklied vom Jammer der Erde" ("The Drinking Song of Earth's Misery"):

> *The heavens are ever blue and the Earth*
> *Shall stand sure, and blossom in the spring,*
> *But you O man, what long life have you?*
> *Not a hundred years may you delight*
> *in all the rotten baubles of this earth.*
> *See down there! In the moonlight, on the graves*

Squats a wild ghostly shape;
an ape it is! Hear you his howl go out
in the sweet fragrance of life.
Now! Drink the wine! Now it is time comrades.
Drain your golden goblets to the last.
Dark is life, dark is death.

If Mahler chose not to call this work a symphony, it did not much help his case in keeping away the Curse of the Ninth. *Das Lied von der Erde* was admired by other composers of the time for its integration of the song and the symphony, making it a hybrid form that history would call a "song-symphony." Many years later, on what would have been Mahler's one hundredth birthday, the great conductor and composer Leonard Bernstein would describe this work to the audience of one of his famous New York Philharmonic Young People's Concerts as "Mahler's greatest symphony."

This twist came long after Mahler's death, but it may explain why fate was no more fooled than his colleagues were by the composer's attempt to disguise this work as something other than the dreaded ninth.

Mahler did live to begin his tenth symphony, but he completed only one movement and drafted four more before bacterial endocarditis—an illness curable today by a simple course of antibiotics—claimed his life. He conducted his last concert at Carnegie Hall in February 1911 and died in May in Vienna, Austria.

Perhaps Death got the last word in fulfilling the prophecy of the ninth symphony curse. Mahler would never hear *Das Lied von der Erde* performed before an audience, as the first public performance did not take place until November 20, 1911, six months after his death.

THE CURSE BROKEN

While composing any symphonies at all still presents a daunting task for classical composers, quite a number of them have passed the ninth mark since Mahler's death.

David Diamond, an American composer who lived to be ninety, composed eleven symphonies in his lifetime. Dmitri Shostakovich wrote fifteen symphonies, and English composer Edmund Rubbra wrote eleven symphonies. Latvian composer Janis Ivanovs completed twenty-one symphonies, Dutch composer Henk Badings finished fifteen, and Alan Hovhaness, an American composer, wrote a whopping sixty-seven symphonies. James Douglas of Scotland has written fifteen symphonies so far, and continues to write in his eighties.

American composer Philip Glass completed his Symphony No. 10, commissioned by the Orchestre Francais des Jeunes and performed by them on August 9, 2012. Now in his seventies, Glass continues to be one of the most prolific composers of our time. Most impressive is the body of work by Finnish composer Leif Segerstam, chief conductor emeritus with the Helsinki Philharmonic Orchestra, who has written a remarkable 270 symphonies and has just entered his seventies.

There are quite a few other composers who have written a ninth symphony and lived to tell the tale, but we have listed enough proof here to feel confident that the Curse of the Ninth no longer plagues the classical music world . . . that is, unless composers believe that it does. Nothing is stronger than the power of suggestion, the belief in potential danger, and the commitment to the self-fulfilling prophecy.

10

DEVIL'S HOLE: THE CAVE OF THE EVIL SPIRIT

Our people in general are ill calculated to maintain friendship with the Indians.
They despise those in peace whom they fear to meet in war.

—Sir William Johnson, British Superintendent of Indian Affairs, 1763

Just down the road from the three towering sheets of falling water that are Niagara Falls, there's a baby ravine with a staircase of three hundred steps descending through a deep, irregular gouge in the rock. As the Niagara River roils outside this treacherous slash in the face of Niagara Gorge—the canyon created by the river's force—hikers and passersby can hear the boom of power, a pounding river's echo often loud enough to stop walkers in their tracks.

It's a fascinating place, an active gorge where the forces of nature continue to play a role. Hikers have found themselves witness to falling rock, and those who do not actually see the boulders fall often have to scramble past stony obstacles left by recent tumbles of earth.

As kinetic as the gorge is, the forces that created it are long since dormant. An ancient glacial lake supplied a waterfall made from its runoff, cascading down the rock face here and wearing away the top layers to reveal the sedimentary dolostone beneath it. Long ago, when the glaciers receded, the native people who lived here believed that the cave-like gash in the Niagara Gorge contained something more than rock, water, and verdant vegetation. They were certain that an evil spirit lived here, guarding the gorge and dispensing portents of doom to anyone who dared to disturb it.

This spirit, the story goes, played a key role in the misfortunes and eventual demise of René-Robert Cavelier, Sieur de La Salle, one of the first European explorers to venture this far into the Great Lakes region of the New World.

I know this particular ravine well, as my husband and I made our way down the long stone staircase in our exploration of the gorge for a number of our hiking books. At the bottom of the stairs, a cave formed by millennia of advancing and receding waters seems to invite hikers to enter, a welcome place to escape the drizzle of splashed surf from the Niagara River rapids just outside the gouge.

Here, we are told, lives the evil spirit, the being that gives the ravine its name: Devil's Hole.

Are you skeptical? Don't take my word for it. Listen to the people much more in tune with the natural spirits: the Seneca Indians who inhabited this land long before the first Europeans found their way to the falls.

LA SALLE AND THE DEVIL'S LEGEND

It is said that the Great Spirit, who gave this land to the Senecas, provided peace and prosperity to them from the day of first creation. When the Senecas began having battles with other tribes, however, the Great Spirit became angry. He decided to punish his cherished people by moving the Great Falls of Onguiaahra, sending storms that ripped boulders away from rock faces and pushing the falls back from its original location at present-day Lewiston. After moons and moons of this violent activity, the falls came to rest in their current location and the great turmoil ceased—but by this time, the movement had revealed this great gouge in the rocks, and the evil spirit could escape from Devil's Hole.

It goes without saying that this huge crevice attracted the interest of the tribe's young men, so one day a particularly daring Seneca man armed himself for battle, climbed down into Devil's Hole . . . and never returned. Some time later, another young man attempted the approach to the evil spirit's lair, and lived—but he could not tell of what he'd seen, because he returned a raving madman, his formerly black hair stricken completely white by whatever had happened there.

The Indian guide who accompanied Robert de La Salle to the Niagara Gorge in the late 1660s related this entire legend to him as they walked. He may have warned that the encroachment of the white man on Seneca soil had already elicited wild sounds from Devil's Hole, shrieks believed to be from the evil spirit himself. The guide meant all of these tales as warnings to the explorer, but he underestimated La Salle's adventurous nature. The Frenchman found the booming gorge irresistible, and one day he decided to descend into it.

To his credit, La Salle did not take any of the eleven men in his exploration party with him, nor did he expect his guide to accompany him. He made the descent alone, without alerting anyone else to his plan, so as not to endanger anyone's destiny but his own.

Wriggling his way down the icy path, he began to hear voices that led him to the murky cave at the same level as the roaring river. When he entered the cave, a thunderous voice began speaking to him in the Iroquois language. While its exact words cannot be known, the legend says that the voice told La Salle to give up his intentions to continue to explore the lands west of Niagara Falls.

"Return to your home in Canada," it implored him, "and long life will be yours. You will have prosperity, and history will remember your name as the founder of a great empire. Go west, and disappointment will meet and follow you until you are murdered far from humans, without shelter or companionship. The eagles of the desert shall strip the flesh from your bones."

La Salle was none too pleased with the evil spirit's prophecy, and he departed from Devil's Hole as quickly as he could, wishing he had never breached the spirit's domain. Before long, however, he convinced himself that the evil one had only been playing on his fears, and he continued to make his way west to seek a passage to China across the largely unexplored North American continent.

La Salle and his men built Fort Conti at the confluence of the Niagara River and Lake Ontario, from which the explorer had easy access to the portage route the Senecas used to get around Niagara Falls. He financed the construction of a ship he christened *Le Griffon* and sailed it to what is now Green Bay, Wisconsin, where it was loaded with furs from the trappers in the area. La Salle remained behind when *Le Griffon* left Wisconsin with some of his men to sail for the Niagara Falls area, but it never arrived—and to this day, its disappearance remains a mystery.

Undaunted, La Salle and his remaining men set off in canoes down the St. Joseph River and on to the Kankakee and Illinois Rivers, reaching the site of present-day Peoria, Illinois. Here they built Fort Crevecoeur, and La Salle left one of his trusted officers in charge while he set off on foot for the Niagara. No sooner had he left the area than his soldiers mutinied, overthrew his officer, and destroyed the fort.

Shaken by this news but still determined, La Salle assembled yet another group of traders and explorers and set off down the Mississippi River, which he believed would empty into the Gulf of Mexico. His trip down the river brought him to several key points that he claimed in the name of France, essentially taking control of much of the land that would be sold to the new American government in 1803 as the Louisiana Purchase. Triumphant—and undoubtedly certain that he had beaten the curse of the demon in Devil's Hole—he returned to France, assembled an expedition of four ships and three hundred colonists, and brought them back to the New World to establish a French colony on the Gulf of Mexico and find the mouth of the Mississippi River.

This last expedition proved to be the most devastating of all of La Salle's losses. Pirates took one ship, another sank, and the third ran aground in Matagorda Bay off the coast of what would become Texas. With one ship remaining, La Salle founded a small colony on the Texas coast and gathered thirty-six men to accompany him on foot to try to find the Mississippi River's mouth. They made the trip three times without success—and on the third try, some of the men decided that they'd had enough of La Salle's cursed leadership. They mutinied, and one of the men—Pierre Duhaut—murdered La Salle.

To add insult to final injury, the colony La Salle had established in Texas fell to a Native American raid that killed the remaining twenty people, the raiders taking five children as captives.

While eagles may not literally have picked La Salle's bones clean in the desert as the evil spirit foretold, the prophecy came true for La Salle in the figurative sense. He met failure and ruin in almost every aspect of his explorations in the west, gave up his land in Montreal that may have turned a healthy profit, and died in poverty and disgrace at the hand of his own fellow explorer.

Such is the tale of the curse of Devil's Hole. This, however, is only one of the manifestations of the wrath of the evil spirit.

THE FINAL BATTLE

Nearly one hundred years after La Salle ventured into Devil's Hole, the French still lingered in the area along the Niagara River, battling the British for control of the Great Lakes. The Seneca tribe worked closely with the French throughout this seven-year conflict—what Americans know as the French and Indian War—and the French paid them for their loyalty by employing them as supply runners.

The Niagara River became the main supply line for both the British and the French, and the Senecas knew how to climb the steep sides of the gorge and keep food, ordnance, and medical supplies moving in treacherous territory. When the Europeans introduced horses and wagons to the portage process, the Seneca runners suddenly found themselves out of their jobs. They began to grumble, and grumbling turned into open hostility.

By this time, the British had won the war, and they began to settle the Niagara area, building a portage road amid protests from the indigenous people who had been their enemies throughout the long conflict with the French. Uninterested in making friends among the Seneca, the British completed their road project and officially put as many as three hundred Seneca out of work.

Bristling with rage, the Seneca reached out to other tribes in the Great Lakes region. Chief Pontiac formed a coalition and launched an uprising that came to its first climax in September 1763.

On September 14, in a carefully calculated attack, the Seneca ambushed a wagon train carrying supplies from Fort Schlosser at the beginning of the portage route to Fort Niagara in what is now Youngstown, New York. They chose the most advantageous place at which to attack the wagons: on a strip of land above the ravine leading to the Cave of the Evil Spirit—the area collectively called Devil's Hole.

Porter Master John Stedman had no inkling that Indians hid in the surrounding forest as he led his supply caravan along this narrow ridge. The cattle and horses in the wagon train panicked and ran, many of them tumbling down into the ravine and spilling wagons, cargo, and settlers into the deep crevasse. As the Seneca engaged the remaining men in close combat, the British had to abandon their muskets in favor of hand-to-hand combat against Indian weapons. In minutes, only three of the original twenty-four members of the supply caravan managed to escape, running on foot to Fort Schlosser to call for reinforcements. The other twenty-one men perished in the battle.

Camped nearby in present-day Lewiston, a portion of the British 80th Regiment Light Foot heard the sounds of battle and came running to reinforce the European lines—but they, too, met with death at the hands of Seneca warriors who awaited them in the woods. More than a mile before the regiment could reach the afflicted supply train, the Seneca leaped on the unsuspecting soldiers and killed eighty of them, leaving another eight wounded.

Later, one of the Seneca reported to Sir William Johnson, superintendent of Indian affairs for the British government, that 309 Indians attacked the caravan and the regiment, and the same 309 walked away when the battle ended. Only one Seneca suffered a wound at the hand of a British soldier.

Did the spirit of Devil's Hole guide the hands of the Seneca as they wiped out the interlopers who stole their land and their labor? The Devil's Hole Massacre makes us wonder what role the spirit may have played, whether he protected his native people from harm during the one-sided battle or helped them keep their aim true. Perhaps he also participated in what followed: the ritual scalping of the dead soldiers and the tossing of their mangled bodies carelessly into the ravine.

In the end, the British won the larger victory. They sent hundreds more soldiers to the Niagara area, eventually forcing the Seneca to cede land along the river to the new colonists and driving the Seneca and other Iroquois tribes up into the land that became Canada. The area remained contentious until after the Revolutionary War, when the new Americans moved in to settle there and began to learn to use the immense power of Niagara Falls.

To the best of anyone's knowledge, the spirit of Devil's Hole receded into the cave after the Indians found new, less hostile places to live. Not much has been heard from the spirit since . . . although to this day, the gouge in the gorge emits howls of discontent in treacherous weather, as if the spirit becomes trapped by wind, storm, and the river's wild current when winter's wrath grips Niagara.

11

THE HEX MURDER AT THE STONE ARCH BRIDGE

What is it about bridges—even bridges that span placid, shallow waters—that make people want to leap from their heights, or to throw things off of them to land hard on the rocky bottom of the river below? Some mysterious force seizes people who stand on the supportive surface above, an inexplicable drive that forces the saddest or the most afflicted to take an unscheduled plunge, or the wronged man with murder in his heart to throw his adversary over the side. Perhaps it's the sense that the water rushing by below their feet will carry away their troubles, or that this powerful current will wash away the sin, the wrongdoing or . . . yes, the curse that has plagued this individual for what seems like an eternity. Trading eternal strife for eternal rest seems to be the purview of the bridge, a structure that serves as a crossroads between shattered life and cleansing death.

Deep in Sullivan County, near the shores of Kenoza Lake, just such a bridge—one with three stone arches—spans the east branch of Callicoon Creek. The bridge has served farmers, residents, travelers, and sightseers since its construction by Swiss-German stonemason Philip Henry Hembt in 1873, and even today it stands ready for pedestrians to cross it, many of them stopping to watch the even flow of water through its solidly reinforced arches.

Here farmers, tanners, millers, and loggers traversed the route between the Newburgh-Cochecton Turnpike and the Callicoon Valley, and lumber workers built a sawmill nearby to make use of the creek's waterpower. Peaceful in the heart of the Catskill Mountains, this bridge provided dependable crossing even to the heaviest loads—unlike its predecessor, a wooden structure that collapsed when loggers attempted to cross with a large wagon full of hemlock.

Here also, in 1882, one of the strangest stories to come out of the Catskills took place. This tale feels like folklore around the edges, but the people involved are part of the historical record—and the grisly murder of George Markert did indeed take place here on the Stone Arch Bridge.

HEX OR NO HEX?

Adam Heidt and his neighbor, Markert, both farmed their land in Sullivan County for decades. They each had immigrated to the United States from Germany sometime around 1857, and now their farms were side by side in the rolling hills of the Upper Delaware Valley. George even married Adam's sister, Caroline.

The similarities between these two gentlemen ended there, however. Scrimping to save enough money while working in a tannery to buy the farm he now maintained, George embraced modern farming methods that made the job easier and produced better crops. Adam clung to the ways of old, regarding everything new with suspicion and even superstition. He and George socialized on occasion because of their familial relationship, but when Caroline died and George took a new wife, their tenuous connection came to an abrupt end. Adam began to regard George in a particularly bad, delusion-distorted light that George neither understood nor encouraged.

So when Adam had a particularly bad year—his cattle were sick, his crops did not thrive, and he came down with a mysterious ailment that made him ache in every joint in his body—he looked for the source of a hex. His mind settled on his former brother-in-law, George Markert, a man Adam labeled as a *hexenmeister*.

Why would George put a hex on Adam? Adam's reasoning is not a matter of public record, but he did know that George had touched him one day, patting him three times on the back. That was the day Adam's pain began. Coincidence? Adam didn't think so, and his was the only opinion that mattered. The worse his luck became and the more debilitating his pain, the more he blamed his neighbor down the road. Adam began to believe that George could re-hex him at any time, doubling his misfortune by doing any simple movement three times in succession. If George stroked his beard, Adam's curse intensified. If George knocked on a door, Adam felt more pain.

Adam shared his suspicion with his two grown sons, John and Joseph. They concurred with their father's diagnosis: George had put a hex on the farm. They saw only one solution to the spate of misfortune—the man who hexed them had to go.

Adam had written letters to George on several occasions, imploring him to lift the curse and end his suffering. The more George ignored—or, worse, laughed at—these letters, the more threatening the tone of the next missive became. A final letter ordered George to remove the spell or face the consequences.

There's no way to know if the Heidts had some idea of how a hex would be cast—though Adam believed the three pats on his back represented a magic number of touches—or how the hex, once cast, would be removed. George, unfortunately, had no earthly idea how he was supposed to remove a hex he was certain he had not cast. He pocketed the letter and assumed the problem would blow over eventually.

When George did not remove the supposed hex, the Heidts decided to carry out their threat. Adam met George in a tavern one night, shared a nightcap with him, and then walked home with him. As they crossed the Stone Arch Bridge, Adam believed he had an advantage, as folklore told him that *hexenmeisters* and others with magical abilities lost their powers when standing over running water. Armed with a club and a .38 caliber revolver, Adam's son Joseph had stationed himself in the shadows at the Stone Arch Bridge. In the impenetrable dark of a freezing January night, they turned on George on the bridge, conked him on the head with the club, and fractured his skull. Weakened from the blows and most likely stunned, George did not resist the men. They completed their dastardly deed by firing five shots into his face and tossing his body over the bridge and into the swiftly running waters of Callicoon Creek.

JUSTICE SERVED

As you no doubt have guessed, Adam, Joseph, and John were not exactly a think tank of superior intelligence. They left a trail of evidence in the wake of the murder: The revolver that matched the bullets in George's body was found under the hay in Heidt's barn, and the threatening letter they had sent to the victim remained in George's pocket even after his body spent several days in the frigid creek. What's more, farmers throughout the area knew that Adam and George did not get along. Justice moved quickly to arrest and convict the guilty men.

John scrambled to come up with a provable alibi and managed to do so, but Joseph spent nearly twenty years in prison on the conviction of second-degree murder. Adam, clearly suffering from some kind of mental illness involving paranoia, landed in the state mental hospital in Middletown, New York, where he spent the last of his days.

And what of George? Dead, of course, the German farmer nonetheless walks the bridge at night, according to residents of the area and ghost hunters who visit. Some say they see him standing on the bridge, gazing down into the water, perhaps wondering how he came to such an undeserved end at the hands of a madman.

THE BRIDGE'S HAPPY ENDING

In 1945, authorities closed the Stone Arch Bridge to both vehicular and pedestrian traffic, leaving it to stand against wind and weather as a relic of a simpler time. The Sullivan County Department of Planning and Economic Development stepped in and began to work on a better solution for the landmark. Their efforts paid off: In 1976, the bridge was admitted to the National Register of Historic Places, and the county raised the grant money to purchase four acres of land on the downstream end and create the Stone Arch Bridge Historical Park. Additional grant money made it possible for the county to restore the bridge to its 1873 appearance. Today you can picnic in the park, cross the bridge, and watch the waters of Callicoon Creek bubble past under your feet.

If, while you're standing on the bridge, you feel a rush of wind, a little lightheadedness, or a bit of vertigo, perhaps it's the ghost of George Markert joining you to watch the waters. Greet him with respect and sympathy in recognition of his empty death and the life he had no opportunity to complete.

12

MURDER IN THE WELL: HAMILTON, BURR, AND THE QUAKER CURSE

Gulielma Sands—Elma to her friends—was hardly a femme fatale or a controversial figure, even by the standards of late eighteenth-century morality. A young woman in her early twenties who had not quite determined that she would live her life as a Quaker, she resided in her cousin's boardinghouse in Manhattan, where she spent a great deal of her time coming down with or recovering from a range of undiagnosed ailments. Her weak constitution often kept her from social events, prayer meetings, and her position in her cousin Catharine Ring's millinery shop, and it undoubtedly caused the moodiness that made her less than pleasant company for many of the other boarders. Even her questionable parentage—her mother never married, and her father raced off to South Carolina when Elma was a child—did little to make Elma the sort of woman who attracted much attention.

So why are we discussing Elma Sands more than two hundred years later? On the evening of December 22, 1799, Elma borrowed a neighbor's expensive muff to warm her hands, slipped out of the boardinghouse . . . and never returned.

Even this mysterious disappearance—a fairly common occurrence in crowded, filthy New York City in 1799—would not have elevated

Elma to notoriety centuries later, were it not for the dream team that defended the man accused of her murder. The discovery of her body, the indictment of another boarder, the ensuing trial, and a curse hurled at the defense team all spelled disaster for two of the budding nation's most revered and controversial statesmen: former US Treasury Secretary Alexander Hamilton, and US Senator—soon to be Vice President—Aaron Burr.

THE CRIME

What exactly went on in the boardinghouse at 208 Greenwich Street (in what is now Manhattan's SoHo district) remains a matter of dispute, thanks to a lack of eyewitnesses and the limitations of medical science at the time. Most sources, however, come together on the key points.

The young carpenter Levi Weeks, about twenty-six years old and gainfully employed in the city, paid no small amount of attention to the redheaded Elma in the fall of 1799. They spent hours in Elma's bedroom talking with the door open, and additional time with the door closed and locked—and the sounds from the bedroom told fellow residents all they needed to know about what went on inside. Boarders would stumble upon piles of Elma's clothing in odd places around the house. Eventually the malaise that possessed Elma throughout most of the year seemed to dissipate, and she became particularly happy, even confiding to her cousin Catharine that she and Levi would marry soon. Catharine, relieved that Elma might soon enter into a legitimate relationship and end her scandalous behavior, did her best to encourage the upcoming marriage.

On the night of December 22, the nuptials seemed imminent. Elopements were common at the time, so when Elma spent an afternoon fussing over her appearance and even went so far as to borrow a fancy quilted muff from a neighbor, Catharine believed that the day had come for Elma and Levi's wedding. Levi stood near the front door as Elma dressed, and no one else was in the entryway when the two took their leave. While Catharine heard whispers just before the door creaked shut, she could not say for certain that Levi and Elma left the house together.

What happened next remains a mystery. A friend saw Elma on Greenwich Street and tried to catch up with her, but someone else called, "Let's go," and Elma vanished into the crowd. Half an hour later, at a few minutes past eight, neighbors reported hearing a woman cry out, "Murder! Lord help me!" near today's Greene and Spring Streets, in an area known at the time as Lispenard's Meadow. Here the new Manhattan Well had been dug just recently, as part of a municipal project to bring clean, potable drinking water to Manhattan and its exponentially expanding population. The brick-sided well had proved to be unsuitable for the planned pipeline, however, so it stood covered with wooden planks in the meadow on the edge of the city proper. (The well is now in the basement of the Manhattan Bistro at 129 Spring Street.)

It was late morning on December 23 before Catharine and others in the boardinghouse realized that while Levi had come home the night before, Elma had not. By midafternoon, Catharine sent a messenger out to a boardinghouse on the edge of Lispenard's Meadow (now Tribeca Park and the surrounding neighborhoods), thinking that Elma might have passed the night there, asking her to return the borrowed muff. Hours later, the messenger returned empty-handed. Elma had not stopped at the other boardinghouse at all.

By evening, speculation ran wild. Had Elma been pregnant and gone off seeking an abortion? Had she not left the house with Levi after all, but with someone else? Had Elma and Levi quarreled, and Elma departed in a huff? Was she lost, or hurt, or worse?

A week passed with no word from Elma, and Catharine's husband Elias, suspecting suicide, hired a man experienced in such activity to drag the Hudson River for Elma's body. It wasn't until more than a week later, on January 2, 1800–the day after a massive funeral procession for former President George Washington paraded down the city's streets, the preparations for which made Elma's disappearance a low priority for local law enforcement—that one of the residents of Lispenard's Meadow produced the muff that Elma had borrowed, found by his son, floating in the Manhattan Well.

With this new information in hand, Elias Ring and his neighbor, Joseph Watkins, went to the well with long poles and probed beneath six feet of dark water. The wooden poles struck a mass; the men hammered together a crude set of grappling hooks and dredged up the sodden body of Elma Sands. Marks on the girl's body made it clear that she had been beaten and strangled before her assailant deposited her in the closed well.

The Ring family made the unusual choice to display the body in its casket on the street in front of the boardinghouse before Elma's funeral, giving friends, neighbors, and other citizens the opportunity to see what had been done to her. It took only a few days before the outraged public convinced officials to arrest Levi Weeks for the gruesome murder.

THE DREAM TEAM

It turned out that Levi Weeks was no ordinary workingman. His brother, Ezra Weeks, was a wealthy businessman who could bankroll Levi's defense—and bankroll it he did. Ezra hired the three best attorneys in New York City: none other than Alexander Hamilton, Aaron Burr, and Henry Brockholst Livingston, a prominent counselor who would go on to become an associate justice of the US Supreme Court in 1802.

Bringing together two rivals as bitterly opposed as Hamilton and Burr could have been a risky move, but the two political figures had managed to work together quite recently despite their political differences. In 1799, Burr enlisted Hamilton's political clout in moving the Manhattan Water Project forward, bringing clean water from outside the city to New York's residents through a system of pipelines and wells. Hamilton, a man dedicated to the principles of the US Constitution—a document he had helped write and interpret through his work on *The Federalist Papers*—saw the benefit of the new water system and did what he could to help see it through.

The greatest clash of the two men's careers would not come until later in 1800, when Hamilton would use his position in the US House of Representatives to help quash Burr's run for president, sending Thomas Jefferson to the President's House instead. Burr would become vice president under Jefferson and never rise to the top seat, a defeat for which he blamed Hamilton to the end of his days.

While Hamilton and Burr differed in their political philosophies, they had a number of things in common—not the least of which was a penchant for womanizing. Famous for their philandering and no strangers to scandal, they may have had certain sympathies for the working-class man who now faced murder charges because of his illicit relationship with a young woman.

Hamilton, Burr, and Livingston would face prosecutor Cadwallader Colden, future US congressman and mayor of New York City. The dream team knew that Colden had no eyewitnesses and little physical evidence to support his case against Weeks, so their job would be to discredit the circumstantial evidence and divert attention to other possible suspects.

THE TRIAL

In 1800, a trial that took two days was a very long one indeed, so when the Levi Weeks trial continued well into the night, it became one of the most controversial and famous court cases in New York's short history. It also became the first trial in the United States to be documented completely by a court stenographer, providing us with a particularly rich account of the proceedings.

The prosecution worked to place Weeks at the scene of the crime, bringing witnesses who had seen a one-horse open sleigh in the area around the well on the night of the murder—a sleigh that fit the description of one owned by Levi's brother, Ezra Weeks. Two men and a woman rode in the sleigh, witnesses testified, and they all seemed to be laughing and making merry. Other witnesses said they saw Ezra's sleigh leaving his home that evening, though no one saw Elma or Levi get into the sleigh, and none of the witnesses could identify the people they saw riding in it.

Colden called witnesses who testified that Elma and Levi had a sexual relationship and that they had talked of a secret plan to marry. Catharine Ring told the jury that she had informed Levi several days after Elma went missing that she knew of the couple's elopement plans, and that Levi had become very upset when he heard that the plan had been exposed.

Hamilton and Burr, meanwhile, directed the jury to consider another possible murderer: a second boarder named Richard David Croucher, who may have had amorous intentions himself toward the pretty, redheaded Elma—a woman of obviously low moral character who would freely flaunt herself to others beyond her so-called fiancé. The defense team claimed that Croucher had been forceful in his assertion that Weeks should be arrested, perhaps insisting too hard that the other man should be prosecuted to cover his own guilt.

Pushing the claims against Elma's virtue even further, they brought another boarder, Joseph Watkins, to the stand. Watkins said that he had heard Elma and Elias Ring making love in Elias's bed while his wife, Catharine—Elma's cousin and employer—was in the country for several weeks.

After this testimony, it was hardly necessary to bring witnesses who said they had seen Levi with Ezra on the evening of the murder. The defense team did this as well, however, further sealing Levi's lack of involvement in Elma's death.

Finally, the defense attorneys deplored the public outcry around the case, saying that this had biased any potential jurors against their client even before the trial began. The prosecution received one last blow at 2 a.m., when closing arguments finally ended—after the defense team waived the right to a closing, observing that "the merits of the case required no summation." Chief Judge John Lansing, one of three judges sitting for the trial, delivered a deathblow to the prosecution when he told the jury that the case against Levi Weeks looked to him to be based entirely on circumstantial evidence. He did not go so far as to order a particular verdict, but he received criticism for decades for prejudicing the jury.

The jury took only five minutes to return with a verdict. It found the defendant Levi Weeks innocent of all charges.

THE CURSE

The story goes that as Hamilton, Burr, and Livingston left City Hall in the wee hours of the morning of April 2, 1800, Catharine Ring blocked their path. Pointing at Hamilton, she shouted, "If thee dies a natural death, I shall think there is no justice in heaven!"

Such moments do not go into a stenographer's transcript, so there is no way to know if Ms. Ring did indeed curse Hamilton in particular, and the team in general, for their role in Weeks's acquittal. Historians suggest that Catharine's curse is nothing more than embellishment of the story, and mention of the curse did not emerge until decades after the trial.

That being said, Hamilton, Burr, and Judge Lansing did see significant hardship in the coming years—not with undue speed or regularity, but in ways that seemed to fulfill Catharine Ring's hopes for their unnatural demise.

The most infamous of these ends, of course, came through the duel between Hamilton and Burr in Weehawken, New Jersey, on July 11, 1804. Burr read in the *Albany Register* on April 24, 1804, that Hamilton had commented at a dinner party that he believed Burr to be "a dangerous man, and one who ought not be trusted with the reins of government." When he demanded a denial and Hamilton insisted that he did not even remember making the comment, Burr challenged Hamilton to a duel. They met in Weehawken, and the shot fired by Burr mortally wounded Hamilton. The former treasury secretary died a few days later, leaving his family scrambling to sort out his complicated and dwindled finances, and to find a way to survive without his income.

Burr was charged with Hamilton's murder in both New York and New Jersey, but neither case ever came to trial. He finished his term as vice president in early 1805 after losing a bid to become governor of New York State, and headed west into the new US territories acquired through the Louisiana Purchase. Burr leased forty thousand acres from the Spanish government along the border of the purchase and set himself up to defend this land should war break out between the United States and Spain. Hearing of his plans, President Jefferson issued a warrant for his arrest, charging Burr with treason. Burr finally came to trial in 1807 and was acquitted on all charges, but his chances for a political career in America had come to an end. He fled the country for Europe in hopes of rebuilding his fortunes, but instead returned to the United States in 1812 under a pseudonym to avoid his creditors. After decades of struggle, he married a wealthy widow who then discovered the extent of his debts and divorced him. The divorce became final on the day he died: September 14, 1836.

As discouraging as these tales of bad ends may be, they pale in comparison to the peculiar disappearance of Judge John Lansing. Lansing's career continued without any major setbacks after the Manhattan Well Trial, leading him to become chancellor of New York in 1807 and the regent of the University of New York in 1814. On December 12, 1829, at the age of seventy-five, he left his home in New York City to mail a letter and was never seen again. No trace of his body or clues to his whereabouts ever emerged. The only hint of his fate surfaced in the memoirs of Thurlow Weed, a prominent New York State Republican, who said he had been told who had murdered Lansing. He declined to reveal the assassins' identities, however, because their family members had become well-respected, upstanding citizens. He noted that the murder had been carried out on behalf of several prominent leaders who felt that Lansing was an obstacle to projects they sponsored.

Henry Brockholst Livingston escaped the reach of Catharine Ring's curse entirely, moving on to a career as a Supreme Court justice in New York State from 1802 to 1807, and to the US Supreme Court from 1807 until his death in 1823. He died quietly in Washington, DC.

Perhaps the most deserving of hardship after the trial for his infidelity to his wife with Elma, Elias Ring met with one setback after another. He lost his boardinghouse when potential residents declined to live in a house beset by adultery and murder, and his household finances declined precipitously as he took work as a mechanic and bounced from one debt to another. When the Quakers turned him away for his "intemperate" use of alcohol, he moved his family—including poor Catharine and her sister Hope—to Mobile, Alabama, where he died of yellow fever shortly thereafter. Catharine and Hope fled from Alabama and chose to live in upstate New York, never returning to New York City.

And what became of Levi Weeks? He fled from New York after the trial and settled in Natchez, Mississippi, where he became a highly respected architect of antebellum homes, including the Greek Revival house known as Auburn Mansion. The home was the first of the famous Natchez mansions and, in Weeks's words, "the most magnificent building in the state," with a striking floating spiral staircase between the first and second floors. Weeks married Ann Greenleaf, and they had four children and enjoyed the life of a genteel family of the early nineteenth century. He died at forty-three—not an uncommon age of death at the time—and his mansion masterpiece has since become a National Historic Landmark. We might leap to judgment here and decide that Weeks should have suffered more for his possible role in Elma's death . . . or we may take his success in later life to mean that Hamilton and Burr were right after all, and Weeks was not the murderer the Ring family believed him to be. Either way, he escaped Catharine's curse. He was the lucky one.

13

THE POWER OF A MALEFICENT GEM

In the National Museum of Natural History in Washington, DC, the Hope Diamond lies in a place of honor—in the middle of the Gems and Minerals Gallery, atop a rotating pedestal and encased in a cylinder of bulletproof glass. One of the Smithsonian Institution's most popular exhibits, the deep blue, 45.52-carat diamond became part of the museum's collection on November 10, 1958, as a gift of Manhattan jeweler Harry Winston.

Any gem of such size and majesty possesses a certain hypnotic quality, and the Hope Diamond tops the list of jewels that have this almost magical attraction. Visitors to the Smithsonian slow their frenetic sightseeing pace to a dead stop when they find this stone. The diamond's fame as the largest of its kind in the world attracts people to this spot, but it's the gem itself, its blue cast sparkling with fleeting flecks of red phosphorescence, that holds people fast.

Is it the glow of this jewel, intensified under light that magnifies its ultraviolet properties, that gives it its sense of mystery? Or is it the tales of death, destruction, and ruin that pursue the gem, from its origin in the mines of India all the way to New York City, that make it seem as malevolent as it is beautiful?

Let's explore the provenance of this magnificent stone, and the curse that traveled with it until a nonbeliever dropped it in a box and mailed it—with just $2.44 postage—to the Smithsonian for permanent protection and display.

A MYSTERIOUS BEGINNING

Where exactly did the Hope Diamond originate? No one knows for certain, although it most likely came from the Gunter district of the Indian province of Andhra Pradesh—or so its first European owner, Jean-Baptiste Tavernier, speculated in the 1660s when he acquired the uncut gem.

How the gem came to Tavernier is also shrouded in mystery. Some say he purchased it from an Indian merchant, while others suggest the transaction was more nefarious. The legend goes that the diamond served as one of the eyes of a statue sculpted in the form of the Hindu goddess Sita, wife of Rama, the seventh avatar of Vishnu. Once removed from the goddess's eye, the stone became cursed—though whether the god and goddess cast the spell or it came from another force surrounding violated Hindu statuary, no one can say.

More than twice its current size at the time—measured at more than 115 old French carats, or about 112 modern carats—the stone was among two dozen or so gems (some tales say it was actually a thousand gems or more) that Tavernier sold to King Louis XIV of France in 1669 for a jaw-dropping fortune of 220,000 livres.

Louis XIV commissioned the court jeweler to recut the rough Tavernier blue diamond so it could take its place among the French court's crown jewels. It took jeweler Sieur Pitau two years to complete the diamond's cut and setting—and he made the gem so spectacular that it captured the imagination, beginning the legend of the stone's power and mystery. At just over 67 carats in 1679, the Blue Diamond of the Crown of France became part of a solid gold cravat pin for the king. Louis wore the stone only for ceremonial events, making a glimpse of it an occasion in itself.

Such a compelling gemstone could not help but take its rightful place among the crown jewels of several generations of kings. King Louis XV had the stone reset in 1749 as part of a pendant worn for ceremonies of the Order of the Golden Fleece, an exclusive order of chivalry established in the 1400s. This time the stone became the centerpiece of a spectacular jewel-studded dragon, surrounded by another 195 diamonds artificially tinted red and yellow. When the pendant passed to King Louis XVI along with the rest of France's crown jewels, Marie Antoinette commandeered the extravagant piece—but, according to historical record, she never wore it in public. As France moved toward revolution in September 1792 and Louis XVI and his wife became prisoners in their palace at the Tuileries, a band of thieves broke into the compound and made off with the crown jewels, including the diamond the people of France called the French Blue.

It's common knowledge that Louis and Marie did not survive the French Revolution. Their beheadings in 1793 have been credited, remarkably, as the first evidence of the dark curse held in the enormous heart of the massive blue diamond. Perhaps when combined with the royal couple's wanton disregard for the health and welfare of their subjects and their love of opulence at the expense of others, the diamond simply pushed their luck over the edge. We could easily regard the diamond's possible involvement as a not-so-startling coincidence, of course, were there not a long list of additional misfortunes that befell holders of the diamond over the course of the next century.

FACT, FICTION, AND MISFORTUNE

After its pilfering in 1792, the magnificent stone vanished from history for twenty years, emerging at last in the smaller form we know today as the Hope Diamond. Exactly what its whereabouts were in the interim remains unclear, but the diamond found its way into the inventory of gem merchant Daniel Eliason of London in 1812, and then into the possession of King George IV of England. When the king died, however, he left behind a debt the likes of which were rarely associated with English royalty. The Smithsonian speculates that the assets of his estate were divested through private sales, and the downsized French Blue, through one channel or another, finally landed in the hands of wealthy Anglo-Dutch banker and jewel collector Henry Philip Hope.

When Hope received the diamond that would bear his name, it had been diminished by nearly 20 carats to its current size—45.52 carats. Hope apparently purchased the jewel for $65,000 in 1830 (roughly $1.6 million in today's dollars, according to the US Inflation Calculator), but Hope brought no attention to his purchase until it appeared in a catalog of his jewelry collection, published in 1839—the year Hope died.

As the diamond became the property of the Hope family, historians began tracking the misfortunes that befell its owners—at least, historians in the early 1900s used this milestone as the starting point for a retrospective of unfortunate events that seemed peculiar to sequential owners of the stone. Two generations after Henry Philip Hope's passing, Lord Henry Francis Hope married an American concert hall singer named May Yohe, presenting her with the enormous diamond for her to wear in her hair. Lord Francis suddenly fell on a spate of bad luck, however, descending into such piteous debt that he had to sell the diamond to pay off his creditors. He sold it to diamond dealer Adolph Weil for the 2015 equivalent of more than 2 million pounds, and Weil in turn sold it to Simon Frankel, a jeweler in New York City, for the staggering sum of $141,000 in 1901 (or $3.7 million in today's dollars).

The diamond sat in the safe at the Frankel jewelry firm for six years, occasionally emerging for a viewing by wealthy potential buyers, but no sales made it all the way to completion before the depression of 1907 hit and the Frankels fell on hard times. This did not stop the *New York Times*, however, from repeating a long list of owners passed around Manhattan at the time, each of whom supposedly bought the diamond from the Frankels and then returned it as their luck went sour:

> Among the stories of ill-fortune attendant upon the ownership of the Hope diamond is one to the effect that Jacques Colet, who

purchased it from Simon Frankel, went mad and committed suicide. Prince Ivan Kanitovski, who had it after Colet, was killed by Russian revolutionists, and Mlle. Ladue, to whom he had loaned it, was murdered by her sweetheart. Simon Moncharides, who sold it to Sultan Abdul Hamid, was thrown from precipice [sic] not long afterward while riding with his wife and child, and all three were killed. It was reported at one time that the Sultan gave it to Abu Sabir to polish, and soon afterward Abu Sabir was imprisoned and tortured. The guardian of the stone, Kulub Bey, was hanged by a Turkish mob. After the fall of the Sultan Abdul Hamid, Jahvar Agha, one of the attendants, was hanged for having the Hope diamond in his possession.

After this stack of claims, for which research reveals nothing that might determine their veracity, the *Times* piles on a few more. It suggests, for example, that Tavernier, who originally brought the diamond to Europe from India, died in Constantinople, Turkey, when he was "torn to pieces by wild dogs." (Tavernier actually died quietly in Moscow in 1689 at the age of eighty-four.)

Smithsonian curator Jeffrey Post, interviewed recently for a PBS program, had this to say about the hoopla around the Hope Diamond: "The curse is a fascinating part of the story of the Hope Diamond that has helped to make the diamond as famous as it is. But as a scientist, as a curator, I don't believe in curses."

Whether the Frankels did or not, they could not deny the fact that their firm fell on especially hard times while the diamond languished in their safe. As the panic of 1907 led to the depression of 1908, the Frankels made a concerted effort to sell what they called the "hoodoo diamond," and the stone found its way back to Paris in the custody of Selim Habib—selling for somewhere around $250,000, or $6.2 million in today's dollars. Habib purchased the stone on behalf of Abdul Hamid, Sultan of Turkey.

With the gem in his possession, however, Hamid began to feel the effects of the curse. Known throughout Turkey for his paranoia, he saw the end of his empire looming large on the horizon and ordered Habib to get rid of the diamond. Sultan Hamid soon succumbed to an insurrection of soldiers on April 13, 1909 (at a coup known, bizarrely, as the 31 March Incident), and found himself overthrown and exiled. He did not, however, ride off a cliff with his family—in fact, when the *New York Times* article ran in 1911, Hamid was living as an exile in Salonica, Greece. He died quietly in 1918 in a palace in the Bosphorus, where he had spent his last days writing his memoirs.

BACK TO MANHATTAN

Pierre Cartier, the French jeweler who owned one of the most respected firms in Paris, London, and New York, purchased the Hope Diamond in 1910. He intended to sell it to Evalyn Walsh McLean, wife of *Washington Post* owner Edward "Ned" Beale McLean, so he collected stories of the diamond's history and wove them into his sales pitch to the McLeans—all the while, however, omitting any mention of the curse. Intrigued by the diamond, the McLeans nevertheless rejected the offer of the stone because of its antiquated setting. Cartier found this an easy problem to surmount: he had the diamond reset in a more contemporary manner, and young Evalyn found the new setting much more to her liking. After considerable wrangling between attorneys on either side of the deal, the McLeans acquired the diamond for more than $300,000 in 1911—the equivalent of $7.3 million today.

When the McLeans later learned from friends about the supposed curse on the wildly expensive gemstone, they took action to attempt to back away from the deal. A March 12, 1911, story in the *New York Times* began, "The interesting circumstance has come out in the negotiations between counsel for the parties concerned in the sale of the Hope diamond to the McLeans . . . that the young couple who undertook to buy the diamond did not know that the celebrated gem had a soul of evil."

The *Times* reported that the McLeans offered Cartier $5,000 to cancel the contract, but Ned McLean had already signed, and the

Manhattan jeweler refused. Eventually, the McLeans relented and purchased the diamond. Reports began to jam society pages of the *New York Times* and the *Wall Street Journal* of Evalyn Walsh McLean's appearances with the diamond in a spectacular, jewel-encrusted pendant around her neck—or, occasionally, around the neck of her Great Dane, Mike. Evalyn used the diamond to create fun activities for children at her parties, hiding it and claiming to have lost it, and then awarding prizes for the person who located it.

No misfortune beyond the norm plagued the McLeans after they bought the Hope Diamond. It remained among Evalyn's possessions until her death in 1947, when her children sold it to pay off her estate's debts. Diamond merchant Harry Winston of Manhattan purchased the stone along with Evalyn's entire jewelry collection. He organized an exhibition of extraordinary gemstones with the diamond as its centerpiece and sent it around the country on tour, increasing interest in the stone and turning the name Hope Diamond into a household term—even providing the stone to an early television quiz show for a special appearance. The diamond finally came to rest in 1958, when Winston donated it to the Smithsonian for permanent exhibition. (He sent it to Washington, DC, by regular mail, insuring it for $1 million and attaching $2.44 postage to the small box wrapped in brown paper.)

Curse or no curse, the Hope Diamond's value is now estimated at $200–$250 million. No bad luck befell Winston or Cartier while they possessed the stone, nor has anything unusual taken place at the National Museum of Natural History since the Smithsonian took ownership of it. Perhaps jewelers and curators have an innate ability to tame its power, or maybe the secure casing at the museum keeps the diamond from working its dark magic.

Or, perhaps, the Hope Diamond has no special power at all, except to hypnotize those who gaze upon it and make them wish for things they can never have.

14

The Curse of
the Black Orlov

On April 6, 1932, a few minutes before 6 p.m., a European diamond dealer named Jan W. Paris stepped out of his twelfth-floor office at 527 Fifth Avenue, stood on the fire escape, and leaped to his death.

The sixty-two-year-old jeweler shared a three-room office suite with businessman George Korper, who had left the building at 5:20 p.m. At about five minutes before 6 p.m., cleaning woman Catherine Casaloff spotted Paris on the fire escape. "She said later that when she had her back turned he disappeared," the *New York Times* reported the following day. Henry Kenny, the superintendent of the building, discovered the body when he heard it hit the roof of a one-story extension between the neighboring bank and the office building.

Paris left two letters on his desk—one to his wife and the other to another jeweler named Charles Sumner. The contents were not revealed to the general public, but Sumner told police that Paris had been consumed with worry over certain business dealings. Perhaps the *Times* reporter did not discover what became clear later, however: Paris had recently purchased the Black Orlov, at the time a 195-carat, gunmetal-gray diamond with origins dating back to temples in India in the early 1800s.

Fifteen years later, two more people would leap to their deaths, each having owned the Black Orlov at some point in their lives. In November 1947, Russian Princess Leonila Galitzine-Baria-Tinsky owned the stone while she lived in Rome, Italy, with her husband. Like many other Russian nobles, the princess had escaped the Russian Revolution in 1917 and fled to Rome, where a sizeable Russian community came together to live quietly in self-imposed exile. Princess Leonila may have counted among her friends another woman of royalty, Princess Nadezhda (Nadia) Vyegin-Orloff, the wife of a jeweler in Rome, who at some point also owned the Black Orlov. Princess Nadia sold all her jewelry to finance her escape from Russia, so she had long since divested herself of the malevolent gem. Leonila may have owned it more recently, though only the Associated Press documents her name and the fact of her ownership of the Black Orlov before she jumped from the fifth floor of a boardinghouse and died on the pavement below.

Inexplicably, Princess Nadia followed suit on December 2, 1947, throwing herself off a building in central Rome. By this time, with three suicides linked to possession of this black gem, the diamond took the name of its third (and so far last) victim. It became the Black Orloff—or, more popularly, the Black Orlov—one of the most dangerous gems in the world.

EYE OF THE GOD?

What makes a diamond, a gemstone revered for its brilliance and clarity, glow black instead of white? George Harlow, author of *The Nature of Diamonds*, writes that the black comes from "numerous tiny, black, plate-like inclusions, believed to be mostly graphite. In some stones the inclusions are so pervasive that the graphite makes them electrical conductors." Recent studies have revealed that the iron oxide minerals hematite and magnetite, as well as some iron, are responsible for the black diamond's dark color. In high concentrations, these minerals can actually make a black diamond magnetic.

Normally, Harlow notes, black diamonds are notoriously hard to polish to the level of brilliance buyers expect from gems by this name. The fact that the Black Orlov achieves the kind of clarity that draws a high price at auction makes it a particularly unusual gem.

Perhaps it's no wonder that people see danger in the heart of a black stone, a diamond that looks as if it has emerged directly from the underworld. While all diamonds form underground, the Black Orlov seems to smolder with power from the deepest reaches of the mines.

Like the deep-blue Hope Diamond, another gemstone trailed by legend and rumors of dark arts, the Black Orlov comes with tales of a shady past. The story goes that a Hindu monk swiped the stone—at the time a staggering 195 carats—from the eye of a statue of Brahma, one of the three Hindu gods of creation. The golden statue stood in Pondicherry, a city in India controlled by the French at the time the unidentified monk pilfered the stone. Subsequently the gem became known as the Eye of Brahma Diamond, but while its name honored its origin, it did not appease the god. Those who traded in precious gems perpetuated the romantic notion that Brahma had cursed the stone and anyone who owned it.

Some authors and critics have claimed that black diamonds did not come from India, so the entire story of the Black Orlov must be false. The diamond industry's leading authority on black diamonds refutes that claim, however, in his book, *The Black Diamond*. Fawaz Gruosi, who is credited with bringing the black diamond into popularity through his venerated de Grisogono brand, writes that black diamonds first appeared in history back in 1671. From the earliest times until the eighteenth century, all diamonds came from India; diamonds were not discovered in South Africa until 1867. The fact that the Black Orlov—then called the Eye of Brahma—appeared in the early 1800s serves as proof positive that it originated in India.

Exactly how Jan W. Paris acquired the jewel or to whom he sold it has become cloudy, but his suicide took place shortly after he came into contact with it. While the *New York Times* did not mention in its coverage of Paris's death that the jeweler had had custody of the diamond, the stone had not yet risen to the level of legend occupied by other such gems—particularly the Hope Diamond—so perhaps no one thought to mention it.

Some of the legend of this stone seems to be mixed up with another diamond, the White Orlov, a 189.6-carat beauty given to Catherine the Great of Russia sometime between 1759 and 1772 by her lover, Count Grigori Grigorlevitch Orlov. (While diamond dealers know that these two diamonds are unrelated, speculation in popular culture seems unable to make that distinction.) Catherine had the doorknob-sized diamond set at the top of her scepter. Using this tale as proof positive that the Black Orlov never came into the Orlov family's hands, the doubters are quick to note that Princess Nadia Vyegin-Orloff did not exist in this time period when Count Orlov gave out diamonds.

These stories about two different gems have nothing to do with one another, except that all the royalty involved happened to be Russian, and two of them were named Orlov.

Even with the objections of those who wish to dismiss these deaths as nothing more than coincidence, the fact that three owners of the diamond all died in the same way makes a compelling story for a curse that began in a Hindu temple in Pondicherry, India.

On Friday, May 13, 1949, New York City jeweler Charles S. Winson closed a transaction to purchase a significantly smaller Black Orlov. An unknown diamond cutter—speculated to be one in Austria—had taken years to cut the 195-carat stone into three pieces, one of which is the cushion-cut, 67.5-carat stone we see today. Winson set the diamond into a brooch of 108 diamonds created by Cartier, hanging from a necklace of 124 diamonds. At the time, he valued the Black Orlov at $50,000 (which would be $487,000 today).

There's a joke among women of a certain age that if you break a chocolate chip cookie into pieces, all the calories fall out, making it perfectly fine to eat. Apparently the mystery diamond cutter's plan in cutting the Black Orlov into three stones followed this cookie philosophy: Once the diamond was severed, the curse would tumble out and disappear.

Remarkably, it looks like he was right. No harm came to any future owners after he cut the diamond.

GONE AND BACK AGAIN

Winson loaned his stunning black diamond to exhibitions, including one at the American Museum of Natural History in 1951, a showing at the Wonderful World of Fine Jewelry and Gifts at the 1964 Texas State Fair, and again in 1967 at the Diamond Pavilion in Johannesburg, South Africa. No further incidents of suicide followed in its wake, and we can only guess that after the Johannesburg exhibition, the diamond languished quietly in Winson's collection. He finally sold it at auction in 1969 for $300,000—a value of nearly $2 million today. When it surfaced again in a 1990 auction at Sotheby's, much of its mystique had faded. It sold for only $90,000.

No one says exactly what happened over the next five years—although Gruosi's introduction of black diamonds to the Western market may have increased interest in these gems and the labor and expertise it took to cut them properly. The next time the Black Orlov appeared at auction in 1995, interest had clearly ramped up again. It sold for $1.5 million . . . and vanished from public view.

Then J. Dennis Petimezas, president of Watchmakers Diamonds & Jewelry in Johnstown, Pennsylvania, stumbled across it in 2004. "I saw an image of the Black Orlov about 30 years ago in California, where I was studying," he told the London *Independent* in 2005. "It was the first time I had seen a black diamond and I became enamoured of it. I was captivated by it. I always read anything about it when the name cropped up and about a year and a half ago, I was visiting a colleague and, lo and behold, it was on his desk."

It took six months of negotiations, but Petimezas finally purchased the diamond for an undisclosed sum. He told the *Independent* that he never felt that the diamond would do him any harm, as its curse had been dormant for half a century. "I've spent the past year trying to discover everything I can about the stone's melodramatic history and I'm pretty confident that the curse is broken."

LONDON DEBUT

After Petimezas secured the diamond, he loaned it to a highly pub-licized exhibition of some of the world's most spectacular diamonds at the Natural History Museum in London, England. "The intriguing legend of the Black Orlov highlights the powerful way that diamonds have captured human imagination for thousands of years," said Alan Hart, curator of the exhibition, in an article on the Natural History Museum's website. "This jewel's beauty and apparent infamy make it a fitting addition to the world's biggest diamond exhibition."

London survived the diamond's visit admirably, although London Metropolitan Police shut down the exhibition because of an immi-nent threat of robbery. The following spring, as reported by *USA Today*, actress Felicity Huffman was approached to wear the stone in its fab-ulous necklace at the 2006 Academy Awards. Once she heard of its macabre history, however, she passed up the opportunity. Petimezas provided the diamond to other starlets for photos, including televi-sion host Nancy O'Dell and then–*Desperate Housewives* star Nicollette Sheridan.

Later that year, Petimezas sold the Black Orlov through an auc-tion at Christie's in a "Magnificent Jewels" sale, for $352,000. This sale provided the capital for an ongoing project he hopes to complete: a trio of objects owned by legendary actress Marilyn Monroe. In a telephone conversation with me, Petimezas said that he owns two such objects: a red lipstick kiss on a Trader Vic's napkin and a lock of Monroe's blonde hair. Both have been laboratory tested and are a match for Monroe's DNA.

"A final ongoing quest is the acquisition of the diamond wedding ring Joe DiMaggio had given her," he said. "All three will make a most interesting collection for auction in Dubai."

Petimezas is justly proud of the fact that he owned the diamond and never came to harm. "The Black Orlov had no ill effects for me; in fact, I had good fortune the entire time I owned it. I married the love of my life, moved into a dream home, and had two of the best business years I ever had."

He did, however, note a single peculiar coincidence: "At the moment the gavel went down on the Black Orlov at Christie's, an airplane crashed into an apartment building right there in Manhattan."

The Cirrus SR20 single-engine light aircraft hit the Belaire Apartments building on Manhattan's Upper East Side on October 11, 2006, at 2:42 p.m., killing New York Yankees pitcher Cory Lidle and his flight instructor, Tyler Stanger. Another ten people were injured when the plane crashed into their apartments, and eleven firefighters suffered injuries as well as they worked to extinguish the blazes caused by the crash.

"A reporter asked me if I thought the two things were related," Petimezas said. "I had no comment on that one."

15

THE WIDOW'S CURSE ON HYDE HALL

Could you ever throw your mother out of her own home? Most of us could not possibly consider such an act, nor could we conceive of a good reason for doing so. Certainly most children come into conflict with their parents at some point or other, but only the most abused, neglected, and betrayed children consider retaliating against the words or deeds of their parents. In those cases, we can hardly blame them.

In the case of the fabulously wealthy Clarke family at Hyde Hall, however, we simply must ask some pointed questions. Why did twenty-one-year-old George Hyde Clarke order his own mother out of the house in 1843—and what consequences did he, his family, and his heirs suffer in return?

THE HOUSE

Hyde Hall stands in the romantically named Glimmerglass State Park on the shores of Otsego Lake on the western edge of the Catskill Mountains. From its doorstep, you can see down Maple Lane to the wooden covered bridge built in 1823, now the oldest surviving covered bridge in the United States. The lake stretches before visitors, glittering in the central New York sunlight, while thick foliage surrounds the mansion and shades its many windows.

George Hyde Clarke, an Englishman, was the grandson of a man of the same name, and the heir to more than 120,000 acres of land in the Hudson and Mohawk Valleys that his grandfather had amassed as the lieutenant governor of New York under the British crown. After the Revolutionary War, the younger George Hyde Clarke came to the new United States to claim his fortune, only to discover that his ownership of the land was now in dispute—tenants who had farmed the land for decades did their best to battle the English interloper for it. Clarke took his case through the New York circuit courts and all the way up to the US Supreme Court, where, after six years of haggling, he finally received a decision in his favor. Clarke could now begin the project that he had imagined for some time: the fabulous neoclassical country mansion that we can still enjoy today.

Hyde Hall, named for the Clarke family seat in Hyde, Cheshire, England, became the home of the Clarke family for five generations. Guests approached the home by passing through a domed gatehouse and continuing by carriage and horseback up a mile-long drive that curved through wooded hillsides and babbling streams. At the time, it may have been the largest country mansion in young America, a place where any family might find happiness and the contentment that comes with taking one's healthy financial state for granted.

Inside, visitors can still enjoy the original dining room table, sideboard, bed, and chairs that have been in the home since it was built. Wandering through the mansion's rooms, you can see tables topped with marble, portraits, books, and even window treatments that are either original to the home's first owners or brilliant replicas, giving us the best possible opportunity to understand the kind of life the Clarke family lived in this wondrous home. The tenders of this New York State Historic Site have even located an 1820s pianoforte and a reproduction of the Samuel B. Morse painting, *A Gallery of the Louvre*, the originals of which were recorded among George Clarke's careful documentation of every purchase and possession.

FAMILY LIFE, FAMILY STRIFE

Before Clarke began construction on the fabulous Hyde Hall, he took a wife—one who brought with her the faint tinge of scandal. Ann Low Cary Cooper had been married to the wealthy Richard Cooper, neighbor to George Clarke's estate and the brother of successful novelist James Fenimore Cooper. Richard was one of the twelve children of William Cooper, who founded Cooperstown.

More than a century later, James Fenimore Cooper II, a descendant of the author of the same name who penned the *Leatherstocking Tales* between 1827 and 1841, would put his own pen to paper in 1921 and record stories passed down through his family about many strange occurrences in the region. One of these tells the faintly tawdry story of Ann Cooper and her marriage to George Clarke.

Richard and Ann, "a noted beauty of her day," were married in 1801. "There are portraits of her still hanging on the walls of her one-time homes," noted J. F. Cooper II in his book, *The Legends and Traditions of a Northern County.* "They show a very handsome, but rather hard and proud woman, evidently of great will power."

Ann and Richard had four children before Richard died suddenly in 1813 at the age of thirty-seven. When we do the math, we discover that Ann was pregnant with their fifth child when Richard passed away.

"There had been much scandal about her husband's friend who owned and occupied a great adjoining estate," Cooper tells us. "The talk was not allayed when, immediately after the funeral, the widow, Ann, went with her admirer to his home. She afterward told my father, a great favorite of hers, that she was married immediately."

Ann married George Hyde Clarke, and Clarke purchased several hundred acres of land adjoining her property to add to his own massive estate. Ann urged him to move along with the project that would define much of George's life: construction of the magnificent Hyde Hall.

"She had in time a son; and then a second son," Cooper relates. Indeed, Ann had a last son from her first marriage, whom she named Arthur Cooper Clarke to honor both the father he would never know and the one he did. She had another son and two daughters with George, naming the oldest son after his father, George Hyde Clarke. (While he did not use a numeral or a suffix, for the sake of clarity we will refer to younger George as George Junior.)

As the children grew up, George Senior immersed himself in the construction of the immense family home. The seventeen-year project began in 1817 with the clearing of the land, and family quarters became livable over the course of 1819 and 1820. George accommodated his growing family and the staff required to tend to them by adding a large wing in the early 1820s. When he inherited his father's English estates and a sugar plantation in Jamaica in 1824, the new acquisitions provided the funds he needed to build a large formal entrance with a larger kitchen and rooms dedicated to entertaining guests. Finally, in 1834, the grand mansion project drew to a close, and George and his family could live comfortably within the largest home in the young United States.

It seemed that the Clarkes had achieved paradise, but all of that changed in 1835, when George Senior passed away just a year after completing Hyde Hall.

George left his family very comfortably well off, so they could look forward to many long years of prosperity. This, however, would not be enough for George Junior, who inherited the home when his father passed away.

"The terms of the will gave Ann the right to live in the house until the son turned twenty-one," said Larry Smith, who serves as coordinator of tours and collections at Hyde Hall today. "But it seems that she was not on the best terms with her son."

James Fenimore Cooper II believed he knew what that was about. He explains that George Junior "married another celebrated beauty and brought her to his home. I doubt if any house is large enough for an ex-beauty of advanced years, and doubtless bad temper, and a reigning beauty, in the glory of her youth."

Jealousy, resentfulness, a loss of her place as matriarch, and any number of other petty quarrels may have ensued, according to Cooper II. "Whatever the cause may have been, Ann was invited to leave and find herself a home elsewhere," he said. "This she did reluctantly, and moved into her father's house a few miles away."

The stiff-necked Ann did not go quietly, however. Cooper tells us, "While the young people stood at the entrance and the horses waited, she turned and with lifted hand cursed the house she loved. 'You may drive me out now, but I shall return and haunt it forever'—were her parting words, as told to me by my father, and the tale runs—unauthenticated, however—that she added: 'May no woman ever be happy in it again.'"

This would all be fascinating, Smith notes . . . if it were true.

"The problem with that version of the story is that Mrs. Clarke was dead in 1850," Smith explained, "and her son didn't actually get married until 1853."

THE PERSISTENCE OF MISFORTUNE

So is there a curse?

Ann definitely moved out of the house abruptly, Smith says, but not because she clashed with George Junior's wife. "One other possibility is that they may have argued over money and his spending," he says. "He seemingly was trying to live the life of a young gentleman, which included things like gambling. Somewhat earlier he had gotten involved with some New York gamblers and had lost considerable sums of money."

If Ann chose to take her son to task for his exploits, it's not hard to imagine that he may have eventually had his fill of her harpings and ordered her out of the house. Whether Ann issued a curse during her last moments on the property, however, may never be known for certain.

Curses usually leave a traceable pattern of misfortune in their wake, but this one did not cut much of a swath. Ann Cooper Clarke promised that women would not live happily in her former home, but there is little evidence to suggest that the mistresses of the house who followed her did not find comfort and contentment there.

There's the dismal story of scandal that plagued still another George Hyde Clarke as he sought the hand of Mary Gale Carter, whose mother so objected to their union that she bundled Mary off to Europe for years and forbade her to write to the man she loved. While trying to convince Mary's mother long distance of the purity of his love, however, George allowed himself to be seduced by another woman who soon claimed that she was carrying his child. The story reached the already burning ears of Mary's mother, who became even more adamant that this monstrous man would never get the chance to sully her daughter. Remarkably, this sad tale eventually reached a happy ending, and Mary and George were married and lived in Hyde Hall—but only after they spent years separated by an ocean and a tyrannical parent.

Ann did promise to haunt the house, however, and some—including Cooper II—do indeed believe that she does. Cooper claimed that he spent a night in the house during a period in which much of the building had fallen into disrepair, one of several times when the Clarke descendants found that the upkeep of such a gargantuan structure exceeded their resources. As an overnight guest, Cooper found himself assigned to sleep in a part of the house that had not undergone restoration from the last time it had begun to decay. (Judging from the hints Cooper gives us, this would have been around 1880.)

"After a look about I got into bed with the candle on the chair beside me, and fell asleep, having no fear at least of family ghosts," he wrote. "I suddenly found myself wide awake, with every sense on the alert and that mysterious feeling, which most of us have had at times, there was someone in the room . . . after I know not how long, I heard a slow footstep as of someone approaching from the corner of the room opposite the door. Slowly, deliberately, it came over the bare and creaking floor, toward the bed; again I noticed that queer sensation about my scalp lock which, as a boy, I felt when passing the grave of the Indian chief late at night."

Finally, the specter approached the foot of the bed. "As I lay motionless and expectant, slowly the bed clothes were drawn across my body, not as if pulled by a hand, but as if someone in passing too close to the bed had brushed against them and drawn them slowly off. Then silence in the room. I leaped from the other side of the bed and lighted my candle. The room was empty."

More recently, stories of spooks in the dark at Hyde Hall have attracted the interest of the television show *Ghost Hunters*, and the historic site itself perpetuates the spooky tales with special events built around the speculated hauntings.

"We have people on staff who swear that they have heard and seen things in the house that they can't explain," said Smith. "It's not like no one has had experiences that they have attributed to ghosts."

Whether Ann Cooper Clarke continues to roam the halls searching for young women to torment, however, may be beyond even the most sensitive medium to determine.

"That doesn't stop us from having fun with it, of course," said Smith. "We pride ourselves on being historically accurate here, but we do get carried away with the haunting and the ghosts."

16

THE CASTLE IN
THE CATSKILLS

On the banks of Beaver Kill (the Dutch word for river), in the fishing village of Roscoe in the heart of the Catskill Mountains, there once stood a small hunting lodge constructed in the 1880s for a man named Bradford Lee Gilbert.

Best known for designing the Tower Building at 50 Broadway in New York City—considered the city's first skyscraper—Gilbert was something of a wunderkind architect, appointed the official architect of the New York, Lake Erie & Western Railroad by the time he was twenty-three. While he lived in New York City, he came from far upstate in Watertown, and no doubt his heart pulled him back into the wooded wilderness whenever he had the chance to get away.

The Gilbert family had amassed nearly a thousand acres of land around the property, and named the estate Craig-e-Clair (or Craigie Clair, as the road across the river is now called). Gilbert's wife, a native of Ireland, chose the name—which translates to "Beautiful Mountainside"—because the heavily wooded area with its emerald slopes, rushing streams, and verdant valleys reminded her of the fishing village in Ireland in which she once lived.

Gilbert could not frequent his beloved Beaverkill Lodge, however, as his work schedule kept him on the road a great deal of the time, traveling as far south as Atlanta, Georgia, to design the Flatiron Building there. He made a name for himself in supervising the architecture of two major expositions, one in Georgia and another in South Carolina, as well as depots in Massachusetts, Missouri, and Chicago. None of this left him much time for fishing and hunting in Roscoe.

In 1903, the Gilberts sold the land to Morris Sternbach, who in turn sold it four years later to Ralph Wurts-Dundas.

A wealthy New Yorker and the grandson of Delaware and Hudson Canal builder and coal tycoon William Wurts, Dundas also came from a moneyed family in Scotland. His discretionary income made it possible for him to fulfill his own desire for a place in the country, a hideaway as grand and as lovely as any he could imagine.

Borrowing from his Scottish heritage, Wurts-Dundas decided to build a mansion in the style of the medieval castles found in Europe, but with all the amenities of early twentieth-century life. Medieval architecture had become all the rage in the late nineteenth century, so there were many examples from which to choose, including a number of castles constructed in Scotland. The dream home had thirty-six rooms, and legend has it that every room had steam heat and electricity—years before anyone else in Roscoe could access or afford such luxuries.

Rumors circulated that the Dundases brought a castle they owned in Scotland to Roscoe, reassembling it stone by stone. Indeed, much of the material used to build the castle came from overseas, so great shipments arriving could well have seemed like pieces from an existing castle. To fully comprehend the grandeur of this estate, we turn to the work of young Richard Barnes, a scholar who researched the construction of the castle. While Wurts-Dundas used local stone from the Beaverkill River, everything else he acquired for the castle's construction came from overseas. "The roofing slate came from England, the marble for the floors, fireplace, and staircase from Italy and the iron gates from France," noted an article written on the castle at the Friends of Beaverkill Community website, referring to Barnes's research. "The fireplace in the reception room was valued at over $5,000 in 1910 [$125,000 in today's dollars]. Gold leaf was used to cover it."

Construction began in the mid-1910s, and towers, turrets, roofs with steep parapets, and narrow, gothic-style windows that came to a point at the top began to rise above the land cleared for the castle. Long, heavy, steam radiators arrived, and one was placed in every room to provide more effortless heat than the massive fireplaces could generate. Stonework to rival the European masters graced each room and the outside walls of the grandiose structure. Pink marble covered the floors and stairs, even on the third floor where such heavy material would require extra labor and careful transport.

While Wurts-Dundas and his wife, Josephine, visited the castle while it was being built, neither of them lived to see its completion. Ralph died in 1921, and Josephine died in 1922 in the Riverdale Sanitarium, a private sanitarium in New York City for the treatment of mental diseases. Here she was one of just twenty patients, most likely passing her final days in one of the facility's private cottages on a spacious ten-acre campus. Thanks to New York State's Mental Hygiene Law of 1927, we cannot obtain more information about whatever illness landed her in Riverdale.

The Wurts-Dundases left the estate and their fortune to their daughter, Murial, but she married a man from Baltimore and never came back to the Catskills. To this day, no one has ever lived in the castle.

An owner who died before he could live in his dream home, a wife with unspecified mental disorders that landed her in a facility for the insane, and a daughter who never returned . . . does this mean that the castle is cursed?

THE STUFF OF LEGENDS

It's true that an abandoned, crumbling castle, a creepy medieval-style estate, and the word "sanitarium" all combine to make Dundas Castle, as it has come to be called, an ominous landmark indeed. It's no surprise, then, that scary tales worthy of campfires swirl around this empty structure's turrets and in and out of its missing windows.

What was Josephine doing in a sanitarium? Some say Josephine enjoyed riding through the town of Roscoe on horseback, lobbing gifts to the children of the village. When the parents of the town objected vociferously to this pastime, they caused Josephine to lose her mind.

So volatile did she become that Ralph and her family imprisoned her in rooms with no doorknobs on the insides of the doors, where she could rant and rave to her heart's content with no danger of escape.

The castle is closed to curious visitors now, but in the days when people could roam through it freely, some claimed to find scratches in the doors and walls of one section of the castle. The scratches, they said, could have been from fingernails, a sign that Josephine attacked the barriers with the only weapons she had to try to claw her way out of her prison.

Some say that Josephine spent her days in a locked courtyard behind the castle—a tale that seems unlikely, given the harsh winters here in the Catskills. Others point to three heart-shaped ponds on the grounds, saying that Ralph had these built to demonstrate his love for his daughter, Murial. On days with a full moon, the story goes, the water in the pools turns to crimson blood.

None of these rumors has a basis in fact, noted historian Dr. Joyce Conroy, who delved deeply into the story behind Dundas Castle. "The thing that fascinated me about the castle is that everybody thinks it's haunted, that people were locked up in the courtyards," she said in an interview with photographer Walter Arnold for his program, "The Mason's Castle: Ghost of the American Renaissance," featured on his website, The Art of Abandonment. "None of it's true. What did strike me as very unusual is from the time that I'm able to record, no one has ever been able to live on that land. That struck me as bizarre."

Perhaps the real story of the curse of Dundas Castle lies with young Murial, who found herself suddenly without a guardian—and fabulously rich—when her father died and her mother was admitted to Riverdale. It became altogether too easy for the caretakers of the castle to take terrible advantage of the young woman, and their schemes removed the burden of much of her wealth. Alone, bereft, and slowly becoming aware of the thievery that had made her fortune disappear, Murial married James R. Herbert Boone, moved to Baltimore, and soon began a fool's errand: the search for "St. John's Gold," a mysterious fortune supposedly located somewhere in England (perhaps related to St. John Chrysostom, who was said to have a "golden mouth" because of his gift for oratory). Murial hired scientists and historians to assist in the search . . . but one day she fired the lot of them, and instead employed a dowser with a willow wand to locate the treasure.

Needless to say, no chest of gold ever revealed itself. People around Murial at the time began to equate her erratic behavior with the mental illness that had afflicted her mother. She landed in a sanitarium in England, and her castle in Roscoe, now in a state of some disrepair, was sold in 1949 for $47,500 to the Prince Hall Grand Lodge of the Masonic Order.

THE CASTLE'S NEW CHAPTER

The Most Worshipful Prince Hall Grand Lodge of New York describes itself as "a non-profit organization which embodies a beautiful system of morality, veiled in allegory and illustrated by symbols. The fraternity, founded upon faith based principles established in the Holy Bible, strives to teach a man the duty he owes to God, his neighbor, and to himself; but interferes neither with religion nor politics as it prescribes the practice of virtues in the conduct of its business."

As a Masonic Order, Prince Hall selected the site to carry out its mission of community service, first planning to establish the castle as a home for the aged. Instead, Dundas Castle temporarily became a vacation spot for lodge members, as they converted the barn on the property into a recreation center and made the old farmhouse their base for administrative operations. In the 1950s, the castle became a hunting and fishing resort, with the addition of a swimming pool, a dining pavilion, and other new buildings. Soon an exciting purpose arose for the lovely Catskill property: a summer camp for inner-city children from Buffalo, Rochester, Syracuse, Albany, and New York City. Naming the new retreat Camp Eureka, the Masons converted the property to the kind of purpose for which they had originally purchased the acreage.

In 2005, Prince Hall and the Open Space Institute (OSI) entered into a conservation easement agreement to protect 929 acres of the property as permanent green space. This means that the land will never be developed as a commercial or residential subdivision, and that Camp Eureka can continue to operate here for as long as the Masons wish. "This historic agreement between the Masons and the Open Space Initiative not only preserves the property and the castle," writes Jane Sokolow for the Friends of Beaverkill Community, "it insures [sic] that generations of inner city youth will continue to enjoy Catskill summers and learn about the environment. Perhaps most important, the agreement preserves and perpetuates the stories and legends of the great mysterious castle on the hillside."

The castle itself is closed to the general public, but if you'd like to get a glimpse of it, you'll find it at 2355 Beaverkill Valley Road in Roscoe. From NY 17, take NY 206 north to Beaverkill Valley Road and turn right.

17

BRINGING *MALOCCHIO* TO AMERICA

Eat thou not the bread of him that hath an evil eye,
neither desire thou his dainty meats;

For as he thinketh in his heart, so is he: Eat and drink,
saith he to thee; but his heart is not with thee.

The morsel which thou hast eaten shalt thou vomit up,
and lose thy sweet words.

—King James Bible, Proverbs 23:6–8

The Italian evil eye lurks just about everywhere in New York State, from Mulberry Street in Manhattan's Little Italy to the bakeries and restaurants of Buffalo's Hertel Avenue.

It shows up every time someone has a headache, a pain in a knee, a back spasm, or an upset stomach. Mention your ailment in a room full of people of Italian descent, and the cry goes up: *Malocchio!* Someone has given you the evil eye. Somebody in your life envies your good fortune and wishes you harm.

Malocchio can pop up without warning, even when people around you actually wish you well. If someone in your neighborhood, at your workplace, or in your family feels jealousy about your new baby or your attractive garden, their thoughts can kill your flowers or give your baby colic. If someone gives you a compliment, and they do not finish the statement by saying, "God bless you!" *malocchio* peers around the corner and strikes you with bad luck for your hubris. Worse, if someone truly fixes you with the evil eye—staring at you while wishing you harm—*malocchio* can strike you with devastating force.

One of the often-told stories of the power of *malocchio* comes from a farm in East Holley, New York, a rural community west of Rochester. It seems that Zia (Aunt) Angellucia, the aunt of the storyteller, accused a farmer named Old Franco of casting his own spell when his cow gave tainted milk. Zia Angellucia suggested that Old Franco must have had a knife in his pocket while milking his cow, which caused the milk to curdle. This made Franco angry, and he stormed out of her house, calling Angellucia names as he went.

Angellucia, incensed at being treated so poorly, put the *mallochio* on the cow. That night, the cow died. East Holley virtually exploded with excitement—could Angellucia's curse truly kill a cow? Several people thought it more likely that the cow ate oleander, which was growing behind a building and would have made the cow sick, or even killed her. The legend stuck, however, and the children of the time told the story well into their adulthood about how Zia Angellucia gave Franco the evil eye and killed his cow.

YOU'VE GOT IT—NOW WHAT?

So what do you do if someone gives you *malocchio?* The difficulty lies in determining who would actually wish pain or misfortune on you. If you don't know who would do such a thing, you will need someone to help you find out—which means that you'd better have a *zia* (aunt) or a *nonna* (grandmother) in your family who knows the rituals for determining who has given you the evil eye, so you can make amends as quickly as possible. It nearly always seems to be a woman in the family who can perform the rituals and detect the person who has given you the *malocchio,* even if she herself does not believe in the magic.

In the book *The Evil Eye: A Casebook,* author Alan Dundes tells of a social studies teacher in North Syracuse, New York, who could cure the ailments of friends and family who had been "overlooked"—meaning that someone had looked at them with the evil eye. Thomasina Pallotta, who passed away in 2005, would attract many friends and family members on her visits home to Naples, Italy, because she was known to have the "good eye," the ability to undo the damage done by the *malocchio.* She did not believe in this supposed power herself, but she went along with their certainty and performed the ritual they requested because she knew it made them feel better.

What sort of ritual is this? Writer Michael Charles describes such an undertaking in an article for the *New York Folklore Newsletter.* He explains that he would take an article of clothing from the afflicted person and run to his Zia Rosa, knocking at her door and blurting out his need for her services before she would let him in.

> The preparations for the session were always dramatic and impressive. First she got a saucer of water and placed it on the kitchen table. Next, a candle was lit and placed next to the dish amid much mumbling and use of the word "Dio." Then she would sprinkle a few drops of oil on the water and, as I watched in wide-eyed fascination, the ritual began. Clutching a black rosary, Zia Rosa began to chant her mysterious words. Rocking back and forth, she held up to her forehead the baby's nightshirt I had brought. She crooned and moaned, and gradually her words because unintelligible. Her huge callused hands made passes above the saucer, and every so often she would yawn (this was a sign that she was getting closer to the identity of the spellcaster). Clutching the nightshirt to her breast, she now began to roll her eyes and shout strange words. . . . Finally, with a great shudder, Zia Rosa stopped all her chantings, and, fixing me with that baleful stare, solemnly intoned the name of the spellcaster. "The one who gave your baby brother the evil eye is Maria Giovanna!"

Knowing the identity of the person who gave the *malocchio* only makes the next part of the task harder. The caster of the evil eye may be a good friend, an enemy, or someone with whom you have no special relationship at all. Whoever it is, however, you must approach them and persuade them to own up to their evildoing, so that you can forgive the afflicter. Your forgiveness lifts the spell—but it must follow an admission of guilt from the person who cast the evil eye.

This can be particularly tricky to achieve. If the person truly wishes you ill, he or she may actually want you to suffer a little longer, and will not own up to casting the spell until satisfied that you have been punished. If, however, the person does not even know they cast the spell, he or she may be very reluctant to accept the blame for thinking evil of you.

How can someone give you *malocchio* without even knowing it? The origin of this belief goes all the way back to the Bible. The New Testament actually explains this in Matthew 20:15: "Is it not lawful for me to do what I will with mine own? Is thine eye evil, because I am good?"

Perhaps it came from a passing thought. An old friend from high school might think something as basic as "I just hate that Adele has a bigger house than I do." Suddenly Adele develops a migraine headache and must lie down in a darkened room for two days. Without a *zia* or a *nonna* to help determine where the *malocchio* came from, Adele may never trace the spell back to the person who had the envious thought. Chances are her headache will dissipate over time, but if Adele never determines who thought of her with envy and never demands a confession, she may be plagued with migraines repeatedly for years.

WARDING OFF THE EVIL EYE

Because it can be so tough to find the spell-caster—especially if you don't have a relative who knows the words to say over the water and oil—people of Italian descent have other ways of warding off the evil eye.

Wearing red underwear, for example—especially whenever you're going to a large gathering of relatives and friends—can protect you from whatever jealousies or mean thoughts may drift in your direction. If you wear your red panties and find that bad things happen to you anyway, chances are you already had the *malocchio* before you arrived at the event.

If the red underclothing isn't practical, or if you just hate the idea of having to protect yourself this way, many Italians, male and female alike, wear a gold Italian horn on a chain around the neck. A gold horn actually imported from Italy will have more protective power than one made here in the United States, but if you're in a pinch, try to find one that was made by a company or jewelry artist of Italian descent.

Descendants of immigrants from southern Italy swear by a combination of the Italian horn and the color red: notably, a plastic red chili pepper horn called a *cornetti*. Carry this on your keychain, hang it from the rearview mirror in your car, or decorate your porch with a string of them. I have it on good authority from my many Italian American friends that these will ward off the evil eye very effectively.

Equally effective, strings or garlands of actual red chili peppers add their pungency to the charm, warding off evil the same way that garlic discourages vampires and other nefarious beings of the netherworld.

Where do you get such things here in New York? Each city of any size in this state has its own predominantly Italian neighborhood, and each of these areas has at least one store that carries these pendants. Researchers Peter Hartman and Karyl McIntosh spent weeks in the city of Utica looking for evidence that belief in the evil eye was alive and well, and they discovered multiple outlets for Italian horns, *cornetti*, and other amulets to ward off *malocchio*. "Virtually every jewelry store in the downtown section offers pendants and amulets for sale that protect the wearer from the evil eye," they wrote in an article for the *New York Folklore Quarterly*. "Small groceries have plastic horns, red peppers, and horseshoes for sale for the same purpose, prominently displayed beside their cash registers. When asked about the amulets' effectiveness, store owners hasten to praise their value and offer a testimony or two in support."

Hartman and McIntosh found that beliefs about what worked against the evil eye and what did not varied between groups whose ancestors came from different parts of Italy—which means that an absolute truth on one Utica street could be absolute nonsense on the next. "Some people wear amulets as a guard against the evil eye," they wrote. "Others protect their home or business by hanging tokens in the doorway. One man told of leaving the imprint of open scissors in freshly poured concrete during the construction of his grocery as added protection against the overlook."

If you're at a family event and you suddenly come face to face with a cousin you know has envied your blond hair or your broad shoulders since you were children, and you left your *cornetti* keychain in your other pants, you can make the sign of the horn with your hand to keep the *malocchio* away. Happily, the sign is very much in vogue these days with rappers and hip-hop artists: Extend your index finger and your pinkie while holding your two middle fingers toward your palm with your thumb. This looks like the horns of a bull, providing enough symbolism to drive away the evil eye. Don't let the person giving you the evil eye see this, however, or the consequences might be even worse.

If you believe your neighbors are sending evil thoughts in your direction, sprinkle salt all the way around your house. This is particularly effective in keeping witches away, because they get caught up in counting the grains and lose their minds trying to find them all. My Italian friends tell me that this is every bit as powerful against evil thoughts and spirits as is the Jewish custom of hanging a *mezuzah*—a tiny scroll from the Torah concealed in a decorative metal or wood holder—on the doorposts of every door in your house that leads to the outside.

Some people make a small cloth sack that they carry on their person at all times, pinned to the inside of a bra or tucked into a shirt pocket. Inside the sack, they place a tiny red pepper or Italian horn or a jewelry charm in the shape of a pair of open scissors, as well as some holy palm from the church. When the bag has been filled, the user sews it shut before inserting it into a pocket or underwear.

If all else fails, hiding the upcoming dates of events that are important in your life can shield you from people who want to give you the *malocchio* to mess up your special day. Whether you are getting married, taking an exam, having a baby, getting test results back from your doctor, or just planning a special evening with your family, telling others the date can lead directly to a curse from a relative or a so-called friend. Keep the date to yourself (except for a wedding, of course, to which you eventually have to invite people) and tell your friends and relations about the event after it happens, and you will avoid the malicious thoughts of those who may want to spoil it for you.

Perhaps most important, remembering to say, "God bless you!" after a compliment always protects the person to whom you've said the kind words. It would be a dismal world indeed if we could not say something nice to a friend or relative without fearing that we will somehow invite the wrath of evil forces to visit them. Thinking of the blessing as a sort of second compliment may make it easier to remember.

Finally, if you have a *zia* who knows the words to say over the water and oil, but she is approaching the end of her days, you can ask her to teach you the chants and the ritual. She can only share this with you on Christmas Eve, however, and only if she also learned the words on Christmas Eve. If there's been a break in the chain, and she tries to teach you the prayers on any other day, they will not be effective when you use them.

As for the water and the oil: Here's how this works, according to Michelle Fabio, an American attorney living in her family's ancestral village of Calabria, Italy, and now a practitioner of the spell to discover the identity of *malocchio* spell-casters. Note that in her version, a pair of scissors is also required to finish the ritual:

> The process is actually quite simple. Place water in a small dish and then drop olive oil slowly into it. If the olive oil disperses, the

Evil Eye is, indeed, present, and you pierce the oil with the scissors while reciting the prayers.

If the oil all comes together in a single bubble, however, you have not been afflicted with the evil eye, and whatever ailment troubles you is therefore your own problem.

Just a note on this: I actually found several references that switch these two oil formations around, saying that the single bubble is the "eye," signifying that the evil eye is present. Your best bet will be to ask your *zia* or *nonna* which one she knows to be right.

Once you're finished with the water and oil, throw it outside where no one will walk. If you throw the water where someone may walk through it, they may get the overlook—most likely in the form of a headache.

THE POWER OF THE *FATURA*

As if a culture needs degrees of curses to put on one another, the Italian community has another, even more powerful way to inflict misfortune on others. A *fatura* (bewitchment) takes a trained professional, someone you pay to cast a spell of bad fortune on your behalf.

The *fatura* caster takes a fee from you, hears your reasons for making the *fatura*, and then assembles and casts the spell based on your specific needs. Once the target begins to feel the effects of this spell, he or she most likely will seek out a different professional, one who specializes in removing such spells. The professionals get paid, the spell is removed, you have had your revenge, and the process wraps up with everyone on either side feeling satisfied. Right?

Wrong. Chances are that the spell-removing professional also can tell the target who cast the spell, and for whom. Now your adversary knows that you had a *fatura* put on him, and he retaliates by putting one on you. You have no choice but to seek out a spell-removing specialist and have the *fatura* defeated . . . but now you're angry at your original target, so you have another, perhaps more insidious *fatura* placed on him.

By this time, you're several fees poorer, you've suffered some misfortunes of your own, and you're in a blood feud that may continue unabated for all time. Better you should stick to the *malocchio*.

18

THE SCANDALOUS CASE OF THE WITCH OF EASTHAMPTON

On a cold February night in 1657, in a settlement called Easthampton on Gardiner's Island—later renamed Long Island—sixteen-year-old Elizabeth Gardiner Howell gave birth to a daughter.

This in itself hardly qualifies as a remarkable event, even in 1657, when births took place in the pregnant mother's home and midwives did the work of medical professionals. But in these early days of colonization along the New World's east coast, anything that went wrong during delivery of a child could be attributed to any number of factors: fever, hysteria, bile, God's wrath . . . or witchcraft.

It would be another thirty-five years before Salem, Massachusetts, would make history with its infamous witch trials, farcical proceedings that ended in the execution of twenty people. By 1657, however, witch hunting had already become a method of swift, misguided justice throughout the new colonies. "The Massachusetts Bay colony, often in a state of religious alarm, conducted witch hunts, rounding up suspected witches—agents of the devil amongst the populace who, disguised as humans, could carry out evil projects—trying them and putting them to death," says an article on Dan's Papers, the mainstay website and publication of Long Island's East End for half a century. "The settlers on Long Island were aware of this practice."

Witch-hunt fever had not reached Easthampton, but the area was ripe for it—and young Mrs. Howell provided just the catalyst the colonists needed to target a townsperson they disliked.

THE TALE OF GOODY GARLICK

In the days that followed her daughter's birth, Elizabeth became very ill, and the friends and family members around her did their best to fight the illness and make her comfortable. They suspected puerperal fever, what we now know as a bacterial infection of the reproductive system—an all too common cause of death after childbirth in colonial America. Several people overheard Elizabeth say to her husband, Arthur Howell, "Love, I am very ill of my head and fear I shall have the fever." She took to her bed, but not long after she rose up in terror and cried, "A witch! A witch! Now you are come to torture me because I spoke two or three words against you. In the morning you will come fawning."

No sooner had she uttered these frightening words than she left her bed and rushed to the foot of it, flailing as if she were in a bare-fisted battle with an invisible challenger. Friends in the room ran for Elizabeth's father, Lion Gardiner, the town's founder and a wealthy, prominent citizen of the colony. Gardiner found his daughter in what looked like a fight for her life. "What do you see?" he asked.

"A black thing at the bed's feet," Elizabeth replied. As she continued to rant, she named another of the townspeople as the witch she saw: Elizabeth Garlick, called Goody Garlick in the custom of the day (short for "good wife," a common term used instead of "Mrs."). The raving Elizabeth Howell claimed that Goody Garlick was "double-tongued," that the woman "pricked me with pins," and that she stood at the end of the bed, ready to rend her limb from limb.

Goody Garlick and her husband, Joshua, were servants of Lion Gardiner, and they were no strangers to accusations of witchcraft. Townspeople had accused Goody Garlick of practicing the black arts, even though she attended church regularly. Considered a busybody and a "naughty" woman, Garlick had already made many of the town's women believe that she could sour a cow's milk, dry up a mother's milk after childbirth, and even make babies sicken and die.

Elizabeth Howell's exclamations became more and more pointed against Goody Garlick. "Ah, Garlick, you jeered me when I came to your house to call my husband home," one account tells us. "You laughed and jeered me, and I went crying away. Oh, you are a pretty one! Send for Garlick and his wife . . . I would tear her in pieces and leave the birds to pick her bones!"

It took nothing more than the ravings of a feverish woman on the verge of death to make Goody Garlick a suspect—and when Elizabeth Howell died the following day, three magistrates came together at the town's meetinghouse to decide what to do. They formed a board of inquiry, and a short time later, they knocked on Elizabeth and Joshua Garlick's door and took Goody Garlick into custody.

Now the floodgates opened with stories of Garlick's practice of the blackest magic. The magistrates took thirteen depositions from townspeople who believed they had some evidence that Goody Garlick had skills in the dark arts.

Goody Birdsall told the magistrates that another neighbor, Goody Davis, had received a visit from Goody Garlick shortly after Davis had dressed her children in clean linen. "Goody Garlick came in and said, 'How pretty the child doth look,' and so soon as she had spoken Goody Garlick said, 'the child is not well, for it groaneth,'" the town's records show, "and Goody Davis said her heart did rise, and Goody Davis said, when she took the child from Goody Garlick, she said she saw death in the face of it, and her child sickened presently upon it, and lay five daies [sic] and five nights and never opened the eyes nor cried till it died."

Goody Hand related another of Goody Davis's stories about Goody Garlick. She told the magistrates that she had heard Goody Davis say "that she hoped Goody Garlick would not come to East Hampton, because, she said, Goody Garlick was naughty, and there had many sad things befallen y'm at the island, as about ye child, and ye ox . . . as also the negro child she said was taken away, as I understand by her words, in a strange manner, and also of a ram y't was dead, and this fell out quickly one after another, and also of a sow y't was fat and lustie and died. She said they did burn some of the sow's tale and presently Goody Garlick did come in."

Story after fantastic story piled up. Goody Garlick apparently could cast the evil eye, making people sick or injured at will. She had animal familiars that went out on her behalf and carried out her black magic. Whatever had gone wrong for anyone in the small town of Easthampton became the fault of Goody Garlick, especially if it happened to Goody Davis.

Do you see a pattern here? Goody Davis told many stories—all through the witnesses that the magistrates deposed. Apparently Davis had disliked and distrusted Goody Garlick since they lived in the same town in Lynn, Massachusetts, along with many of their current neighbors. She herself never testified, for reasons that are not clear in the records, but the pattern of testimony coming from her did not escape the notice of the magistrates—or of Lion Gardiner, the father of the victim, Elizabeth Gardiner Howell, and the employer of many people in Easthampton.

Gardiner was not asked to testify in the case, but he provided information that he knew would be of interest to the court. This went into the record: "It is creditably reported by a local Authority, that Mrs. Garlick had been employed in the Family of Capt. Lyon Gardiner, and that another Woman in the same Employ had accused Mrs. Garlick of causing the Death of her Child; while, according to Capt. Gardiner, the Woman who had been a Witness against Mrs. Garlick, had taken an Indian Child to nurse, and starved her own Child to Death for the Sake of the Pay she was to receive for supporting the Indian Child."

These grim facts certainly would be important in the upcoming trial. The mounting evidence, such as it was, began to worry the magistrates about their ability to tell fact from fiction and coincidence from witchcraft. Once they completed their depositions and considered the ramifications of a witch trial in their jurisdiction, these community leaders decided that they should send the case to a court that had much more experience with trials of this nature. *The Annals of Witchcraft in New England* confirms that "the Magistrates after hearing the Testimony, and not being skilled in the Science of Demonology, concluded to send the Accused to the General Court of Connecticut, in which the occult Doctrine would probably be more safely applied."

THE TRIAL OF GOODY GARLICK

Off the case went to Hartford. The court here had tried many witch cases and had convicted and executed a number of defendants, so there was no way to predict which way it might swing for Easthampton's very own witch.

The Hartford colony had a new governor: John Winthrop Jr., a reasonable and learned man who did not put much stock in tales of sorcery and spells. He brought to the bench a healthy skepticism of the testimony put before him, believing that if the devil's work did take place on earth, commoners in the Massachusetts Bay Colony probably did not have the power to carry it out.

A scholar and a researcher, Winthrop spent his own time working to explain the natural phenomena he witnessed around him and the origins of such forces. He had the unusual ability to see beyond the day's hype and hysteria and look for the logical sources of things attributed to black magic. In this way, Winthrop stands as one of the first sociologists, looking to dispel panic and replace it with a better understanding of the workings of crowds, communities, and interpersonal relations.

We can't know exactly what went on in the Hartford courtroom when Goody Garlick came to trial because records of court proceedings were not kept until the early 1800s, but we do know that Goody Garlick was acquitted. The court's directive to the community of Easthampton, however, is a matter of public record:

> It is desired and expected by this court that you should carry neighborly and peaceably without just offense, to Jos. Garlick and his wife, and that they should do the like to you.

Goody Garlick went home to Easthampton, and found that the townspeople were willing to follow Governor Winthrop's directive. They lived out their lives peacefully in the town, side by side with their one-time accusers, and their son grew up to be the town's miller, a post that carried some clout and deference.

No more cases of witchcraft came out of the town once the Garlick case closed. Visitors to the town today can see Lion Gardiner's original home on Main Street, as well as the Gardiner windmill that once powered the milling industry, and a number of carefully preserved buildings from the time when people believed that the dark arts could be practiced in the little house next door.

19

"WICKED AND DETESTABLE ARTS" IN SEATALLCOTT

You don't hear a great deal of talk about witchcraft in seventeenth-century New Netherlands, the colonies that eventually became New York State. The Dutch, who settled these colonies beginning in the late 1500s, had already matured beyond the hysteria over the existence of witches that still plagued England and other countries throughout the European continent. Magistrates and other leaders in colonial law who came to the New World from Holland took the bench with a predisposition against claims of witchcraft, and they made it fairly clear to people who brought such claims that they would be regarded with skepticism at best, and with questions about their own mental stability at worst.

In 1664, however, a new population of settlers joined the Dutch in the colonies along eastern Long Island. Huguenots (French Protestants), Scandinavians, some English, and their African slaves all arrived to make the budding towns along the outskirts of the island their home, bringing with them their own cultural differences, their religious beliefs, and their superstitions.

In this legal climate, a strange case about which little is known did come before the New York courts on Long Island in October 1665, at the Court of Assizes. "The Tryall of Ralph Hall and Mary his wife, upon suspicion of Witchcraft" came before a jury of twelve men on October 2.

The indictment against these two townspeople of Seatallcott (which became present-day Setauket) read as follows: "That Ralph Hall of Seatallcott aforesaid, upon the 25th day of December, being Christmas day last was 12 months . . . by some detestable and wicked Arts, commonly called Witchcraft and Sorcery, did (as is suspected) maliciously and feloniously, practice and Exercise at the said towne of Seatallcott in the East Riding of Yorkshire on Long Island aforesaid, on the Person of George Wood, late of the same place, by which wicked and detestable Arts, the said George Wood (as is suspected) most dangerously and mortally sickened and languished. And not long after by the aforesaid wicked and detestable Arts, the said George Wood (as is likewise suspected) died."

The indictment goes on to say that Ralph Hall used his same "wicked and detestable Arts" on the infant child of George Wood's widow, Ann Rogers, until the child "sickened and languished, and not long after . . . died." The same indictment was read against Mary Hall, Ralph's wife, accusing both townspeople of murder.

What was the motive? Sadly, the transcript of the trial does not tell us this, as there were no witnesses who testified in person during the proceedings. The attorneys involved did take a number of depositions before the trial, and these were read—but their contents are not part of this bill of indictment, so we are not likely to learn what clues led townspeople to believe that George Wood and his child were murdered by "wicked and detestable Arts."

This gap in the history of the trial inspired author Edward V'Kanty to take a stab at reconstructing the incidents leading to the deaths of George Wood and his infant child in his 2015 historical novel, *Testament: The Trial.* V'Kanty suggests that the Halls had designs on the land on which George Wood had just constructed a house for his family. The novel goes to fantastical lengths to paint Ralph and Mary Hall as true witches, exercising magical powers and using incantations and bloody rituals that result in the deaths of both George Wood and his infant son from a mysterious, multi-symptom illness.

The missing depositions must not have been nearly as strong as V'Kanty's novelization, however, because the jury came back with the following verdict: "We having seriously considered the Case committed to our Charge, against the Prisoners at the Barr, and having well weighed the Evidence, we find that there are some suspicions by the Evidence, of what the woman is Charged with, but nothing considerable of value to take away her life. But in reference to the man we find nothing considerable to charge him with."

The court, satisfied with the innocence of the Halls, gave this sentence: "That the man should be bound Body and Goods for his wives Apperance, at the next Sessions, and so on from Sessions to Sessions as long as they stay within this Government, In the meanwhile, to be of their good Behavior."

The Halls were released on their own recognizance, and they did not find themselves in court again after that.

What can we assume from this account? Is it possible that Ralph and Mary Hall did indeed send some kind of evil curse or spell in the direction of George Wood and his child—one so powerful that it could kill them both? If such a thing were possible, as so many cultures believe (but not, remarkably, the Dutch government that ran the local court), could the Halls have perpetrated such a subtle curse that testimony describing it could be disregarded so easily?

The Penguin Book of Witches, as good an authority as any on the subject, notes that this was the only prosecution for witchcraft to be tried in the court of this early government of New York: "Although the Dutch are considered as superstitious, yet they invariably dismissed all complaint proffered for this alleged offence . . . and they published all attempts to introduce superstition by publicly alarming the populace. . . . This solitary instance of a prosecution for witchcraft did not originate in that part of the colony settled by the sober burghers from the Naderlandt, but among the emigrants from Connecticut and Massachusetts on the eastern part of Long Island, and it is fair to presume that if the majority of the jury had not been Dutchmen it would have gone hard with poor Ralph Hall and his wife. Many were executed in New England against whom the case was nothing like as strong as this."

20

THE KNICKS, THE RED BULLS, AND THE WORST LUCK IN SPORTS

et me begin here with two apologies. First, I apologize to sports fans for emphasizing the astronomical amount of bad luck the sports franchises in New York State have when it comes to winning a championship—but there it is, and I can't ignore it while I'm writing a book called *Cursed in New York*. Second, for those who picked up this book expecting lots of tales of ghosts and other phenomena of the paranormal, I wish I could accommodate you. The fact is that our ghosts generally hang around New York out of their own interest, not so much because they wish to inflict harm on others. (But stay tuned—the next two chapters should satisfy your craving for cursed spirits.)

The supernatural forces that hate New York sports, however, are alive, well, and having the times of their lives here in the Empire State. If you don't believe me, I give you the Ewing Curse, the lingering preventative that stands between the New York Knickerbockers (our National Basketball Association franchise) and even one championship win since 1973.

Remember the Knicks? Back in the early 1970s, they were the team to beat, led by coach Red Holzman and grabbing two championship wins in 1970 and 1973. In 1972 they made it to the NBA finals as well, making fans believe that they had a terrific, winning future ahead of them. A series of tepid to losing seasons followed, however, and by 1985, the team found itself in the first-ever NBA Draft Lottery.

Not all NBA teams participate in the lottery. It's for the teams that have missed the playoffs in the previous season, to determine in what order the teams will choose new players from college basketball players across the United States (as well as some international players). The fourteen teams that do not make the playoffs enter into the lottery to become one of the top three to choose new players. The team with the worst record has the best chance to get a higher draft pick, giving this team the opportunity to get the best new player and increase its competitiveness in the coming season. After the first three picks, the rest of the teams are slotted in according to their win-loss record, with the team with the most losses going first.

Before 1985, teams would simply line up for the draft, with the team with the most losses in the previous season going first. The worst teams in each division would flip a coin to see who got the first draft pick, and the other teams would fall into line behind these two in order of their loss record. Can you see the problem? In 1984, accusations flew that the Houston Rockets, who won the coin toss, had deliberately lost games to get a better position in the draft. The NBA countered this talk by introducing the lottery system, making a team's position in the lottery more of a question of chance than of strategy.

So, in 1985, the New York Knicks won the lottery draw and got their first pick of the draft candidates. They chose Patrick Ewing, to this day one of the most valuable rookies ever to play professional basketball.

And inexplicably, that's when things started to go wrong.

WAS THE FIX IN?

No one can say for certain, but there's a belief among some NBA players at the time—and fans who were paying close attention—that some kind of draft rigging took place. Some people commented that the card Commissioner David Stern pulled with the Knicks' name on it had a bent corner. Why would the drawing be rigged? Despite their dismal record over the last several years, the New York Knicks were still the most profitable team in basketball. Giving them a boost to get them back into championships would mean a big increase in their bottom line, which would mean profits for everyone.

Ewing had one of the most successful careers in basketball, as every fan knows, but he couldn't convert the Knicks to a championship-winning team. In the 1990s, the Knicks made it to the playoffs in eight straight years, but they couldn't put it over the line and win their way into the finals.

The near-miss 1990s led to the dismal 2000s, when the Knicks had some of the most embarrassing seasons in their history. While the Ewing curse was an elbow-in-the-ribs, "in" joke in the 1990s as the team lost one playoff game after another, the decades since the turn of the millennium have made fans wonder much more seriously if a little sleight of hand in the 1985 lottery really could cause a shower of perpetual bad luck over Madison Square Garden's original team for eternity.

RED BULLS FINALLY CHANGE THEIR LUCK

Back in 1996, when the New York Red Bulls major league soccer team went by the name New York/New Jersey MetroStars, the team played its very first home game in Giants Stadium in East Rutherford, New Jersey. Forty-six thousand excited fans attended this inaugural game, hinting at the enthusiasm with which soccer (football to the rest of the world) had come to the United States, a country that lagged behind most of the world in its interest in this particular sport.

That first season's team included stars from all over the world: Tab Ramos, who played in Spain and Mexico before joining the Metro-Stars; World Cup players Tony Meola and Peter Vermes; a Venezuelan named Giovanni Savarese; Roberto Donadoni from Milan, Italy; and another Italian, Nicola Caricola (pronounced like "curricula"–this will become important in a moment), as well as a roster of relatively unknown players including Andrew Restrepo, Jeff Zaun, and Edmundo Rodriguez. Given the team's impressive lineup and its backing by the city of New York and the state of New Jersey, soccer fans across the nation assumed that the MetroStars would soon become the top team in the brand-new Major League Soccer (MLS) organization.

At that first game, however, with only a few hours' competitive play behind them, the MetroStars took a turn toward a dark and dismal place.

With a tied score of 0–0 and just seconds left in this first home game, the match was about to go into "shootout." A shootout is a tie-breaking penalty-kick competition in which each team takes five shots from the penalty mark, with the net defended only by the goalkeeper. The team scoring the most goals then becomes the winner.

The MetroStars were about to celebrate their shutout play to this point when a player from the opposing team, the New England Revolution, kicked a ball toward the MetroStars' net. Nicola Caricola, playing defense, stopped the ball with a kick of his own . . . but instead of going back out onto the field, the ball shot away from him in the opposite direction, rolling at top speed into the MetroStars' net. Caricola had scored an "own goal" for New England.

The game ended a few seconds later, with the entire MetroStars team staring in disbelief at the scoreboard. (If you want to live this horror along with Caricola and see his face at the moment he realized what he had done, you can find the video of it on YouTube.)

Anyone can make a mistake, but as one game became a season and one season became five, ten, and so on, the team could not push its way past what fans began to call "The Curse of Caricola."

"The curse . . . it's a great story," says Mike Petke, a former Metro-Stars player who served as the team's head coach in 2013 and 2014. Petke appears in a video that documents the supposed curse. "Do we believe in magic? Do we believe in voodoo? Are we really sitting here saying that a player cursed us?"

Indeed we are, the fans responded, as one playoff opportunity after another went awry on the field. In 2000, just after scoring what should have been the winning goal in the third game of the championship, the referee dropped a flag on the play, disallowing the goal. In 2008, the New York Red Bulls (renamed in 2006 when Red Bull GmbH bought the team) narrowly missed another playoff win, and in the Eastern Conference Semifinals in 2012, the ref called encroachment when Red Bull players began to run offside before penalty kicker Kenny Cooper took what would have been the winning kick. Cooper had to take the kick again, and the goalkeeper blocked it neatly.

Does such a curse live forever? Mike Petke decided otherwise. "No, I don't believe in the curse," he said in the video mentioned earlier. "I believe that we get what we put in."

Putting his faith in the team rather than in the Curse of Caricola, Petke led the team to improve their defensive play and fight their way to a two-month winning streak in 2013, making them the best team of the season. The Red Bulls received their first-ever piece of "silverware," the Supporters' Shield, at the end of the regular season.

While the team still has not secured the MLS Cup as of this writing, sports media and players alike have declared the curse broken.

"For once the Red Bulls' demons had left themselves too much to do, and just like that the 'curse' was lifted," proclaimed writer Graham Parker in the *Guardian* the next morning. "For Sunday night . . . [Petke] was happy to toast Caricola ('poor guy . . . I hope he's enjoying a coffee and a cigarette back in Italy') and relish the fact that at 37 he'd become the youngest head coach to win a Supporters' Shield—and the only one from New York."

21

THE FARMER, THE BEGGAR, AND THE PEACH ORCHARD

This is a story with a moral, in the good, solid tradition of Aesop and the Brothers Grimm. It comes to us from descendants of the farmer to whom this happened, through the wonderful New York Folklore Society, which collects such tales and publishes them in a quarterly magazine.

Is it true? We can say that it's as true as any folk tale, once a family has told and retold it for several generations.

John Hicks farmed land left to him by his father, the kind of land that allows a farmer to make excellent use of the rich soils of the Hudson Valley. Each year, as his profits allowed, Hicks bought additional land adjoining his acreage, adding pasture, woodlands, and more livestock.

The more land he had, the more he could produce crops and cattle that netted him nice profits at market. He expanded the farmhouse he shared with his wife, making it one of the most nicely cared for properties in his area. People would comment as they passed on the country road, saying, "Hicks must be doing well."

No one would say that Hicks deserved his good fortune, however, because he was known in town and for miles around as a bitter, covetous man who would sooner save himself a penny than help his fellow man. They did like his wife, however, considering her a fine woman with a kind and generous heart.

One spring, Hicks tilled some of his acreage and planted 350 peach trees. Over the years, as the saplings matured and became ready to bear fruit, he tended to them as if they were his own children—and this was just as well, because he had no children and needed something he could care for so tenderly. Five years passed before the peach trees finally showed signs of bearing fruit. Tiny pink buds appeared at the ends of the branches, ready to burst into bloom on the first warm day of spring. Leaves sprouted, turning from the light green of new growth to the deep emerald of summer. It looked like all of Hicks's hard work would pay off that year, and he would have many fine peaches to take to market.

One Sunday morning, as Farmer and Mrs. Hicks were enjoying their breakfast, they heard a knock at their door.

John Hicks answered the door and gruffly acknowledged a man of about his age standing there. The man's clothing was old and patched but clean, and his shoes were dusty and scuffed from many miles of walking. He looked pale and tired, though he greeted Hicks with a smile.

"Good morning, sir. Could I trouble you for a cup of coffee and a bite of food? I have walked many miles, and I have not eaten since yesterday morning."

Mrs. Hicks quickly rose from the table to get another plate, but her husband stopped her. "Sit down," he barked in her direction. She stopped but did not sit.

"Why should I feed you with food from my table?" Hicks responded, furrowing his eyebrows at the man at his door. "I have worked for my keep. I am in the fields from dawn to sundown day after day, every day of the year. I milk my cows and I feed my livestock. Even on Christmas, I must work to make my living. You come begging, as if you deserve a handout. Be off with you."

"But sir," the man replied, "I am not just a beggar. I always worked for my keep, for many years. Recently I have had a terrible illness, and my employer could not hold my job for me for so many months. I am better now and I have a new job in the next town. I have been walking for two days to get there. Yesterday some of your neighbors, in a cottage well down the road, gave me bread, milk, and some meat from their table when I stopped there. In my heart, I blessed their house. I would be happy to do the same for you."

Again Mrs. Hicks started for the larder, but her husband raised his hand. "You are a lazy slug-a-bed," he told the man, "and I do not believe that the blessing of such a man will have any effect. My farm is already healthy and prosperous, thanks to the work of my own hands. Be off, and do not beg at my door again."

Hicks was about to close the door in the man's face, when the man raised his hand as if it were a claw. Hicks could not explain why, but the strange gesture made him go cold from his forehead to his feet. He stood motionless as the man spoke.

"I see your beautiful peach orchard in bloom. Now I curse that orchard. Every bud will blacken and die, and every leaf will wither and fall to the ground. You will never see a peach from this orchard, not ever. And the blight will come soon."

The man lowered his hand, and the blood seemed to begin to flow again in Hicks's body. His wife, behind him, trembled and clutched the back of a chair.

Without another word, the man turned on his heel and walked away. Further down the road, he walked up to another door, where he was greeted with smiles and a place at the family's table on that beautiful Sunday morning.

For the next several days, Hicks did his best to forget about the man and his strange curse. He could not deny, however, that his beautiful peach orchard was starting to look a little sad. The leaves on the trees began to yellow and curl. The petals fell from the flowers, covering the ground with tiny satiny dots, but no tiny balls of fruit replaced them. Soon the leaves, now spotted with blight, began to fall as well.

By the end of the week, the trees were bare, and no fruit emerged from the buds that had been so promising just a few days earlier.

There was no way to explain this sudden, complete loss of his expected peach crop. New York can be a tough place to grow peaches and other stone fruit, but there had been no cold snap that week, and if the brown rot or cankers had come to his orchard, it would have come to others in the area as well. He saw no insects among his peaches except for the bees, which seemed as baffled as he. His neighbors' orchards were healthy and full of blooms and swelling fruit. Only his peach trees, the growth of five years of hard work, had shriveled and given up.

"That man," he said to himself over and over. "That man."

For his selfishness with a bit of bread and milk, he had squandered half a decade of effort.

To his own surprise, a verse from the Bible leaped into his mind, even though he had not been to church for many decades. "For I was hungry and you gave me nothing to eat," the words echoed in his head. "I was thirsty and you gave me nothing to drink, I was a stranger and you did not invite me in, I needed clothes and you did not clothe me, I was sick and in prison and you did not look after me."

He could not remember what passage this was, but when he asked Mrs. Hicks, she told him readily—it was Matthew 25:42–43, and she finished the chapter with the words of the king: "Truly, I tell you, whatever you did not do for one of the least of these, you did not do for me. Then they will go away to eternal punishment."

The peach orchard never bloomed again.

Now for the promised moral: Open your heart and help the hungry man—not just because you will be rewarded in the hereafter, as that may not be your belief, but also because it is the right thing to do. If you harden your heart to the person who has nothing, woe will come to you. The universe balances itself out; be on the right side of it.

22

THE LEGEND OF
THIRTEEN CURVES

Cedarvale Road, ten miles west of Syracuse in the town of Onondaga, bends back and forth thirteen times through thick woods as it follows an unnamed creek. Thanks to this remarkable topography, many locals hardly know the official name of this segment of County Road 42. They know it only as Thirteen Curves.

Young drivers love to cruise this road on dark nights, especially on Halloween. They come in search of a filmy apparition that only the luckiest can see: a young woman in a white wedding dress, often spattered with her own red blood, crossing the road near the creek in her eternal search for her husband.

It is said that an accident seventy years ago or more took the lives of this bride and her husband of only a few hours as they drove away to begin their planned honeymoon. The husband took one of the curves with great speed and lost control of the car, sending the vehicle crashing down a ravine and into the creek bed. The groom died instantly when his head was severed from his body.

The bride, somehow surviving the terrible accident, picked up the groom's head and began to walk, searching for anyone who could help her. She came upon a local farmer, but her strength and will to live gave out just as she reached him, and she collapsed and died at the man's feet.

No one knows the names of these two unlucky souls, so there is much speculation about the couple, their conveyance, and the manner in which they died. Some suggest that the tale is really much older than seventy years—that it predates the automobile, and the couple actually rode in a horse-drawn carriage. When an animal or another surprise in the dark spooked the horses, they reared and ran off the road into the forest. The carriage splintered as it ran into trees and rocks in the surrounding woods, and the couple flew out of the carriage and died as they slammed into the ground.

Another version suggests that the groom came from a well-to-do family, so he drove a 1940 Packard Super Eight limousine, reportedly the finest car on the road at the time of the accident—though not equipped with safety features that could have saved the two young souls. One legend suggests that the groom was drunk, making this a cautionary tale for today's young drivers who bring beer while they cruise this road looking for the ghost he left behind. Still another reports that the whole scene happened on a perilously snowy Syracuse night, sending the couple sliding into icy waters with no hope of regaining control of their vehicle.

Others say that only the groom lost his life at Thirteen Curves, leaving the bride to live out her life alone. Today she haunts this spot in search of her lost love, returning in death to the age and appearance of a newlywed as she waits for the spirit of her husband to find her. Adding more fuel to this stoked tale, some say it's the other way around—that the bride died but the groom walked away from the crash, and the bride's spirit remains, forever searching for the love she left behind.

Whatever her origin, the ghost is cursed to repeat a pattern of behavior night after night, most often on any Friday the thirteenth—the speculated date of the accident that took her husband's life, and perhaps hers as well—and on October 31, when ghosts celebrate All Hallows' Eve by increasing their visibility.

How does the cursed bride appear? A commenter who goes by the handle MsMaryMac describes it on the Weird U.S. website: "While making our way around the sixth curve, a dim glowing white shape appeared in the road ahead of us. It slowly made its way from the left side of the road to the right. When it got right in the middle of the road, it stopped and turned towards us. It was about the height of an average woman, but it was not very well defined—it was more of a staticy [sic] blur than a clear image. It did have a red glow up near where the head would approximately be on a human being."

MsMaryMac was lucky to get away from Thirteen Curves with such a sighting. Many who search for the phantom bride believe that she has a vindictive streak, popping out of nowhere in a flash of light to cause others to crash and die the way she did all those years ago.

Many other brave souls who have driven the treacherous road on the right day at the right time (midnight, of course) say that the bride suddenly appears in the rearview mirror, sitting in the backseat of their car. This is when the spattered blood on her gauzy wedding dress becomes visible, though if the driver or passenger turns around to look more closely, the vision dissipates and the ghost disappears.

Others see her face in the passenger-side window, peering into the car to find someone who can help her locate her husband.

Some say the accident took place near the seventh curve—the tightest and most dangerous curve on the road, nicknamed "Dead Man's Curve" by locals who frequent the area. One source of this information comes from an article by Frederic Pierce on the Syracuse. com website, in which Pierce's youngest son explains that the bride "had been a friend of his friend's great grandfather, and that's probably a reliable source." The next day, however, Pierce posted a new piece "unveiling" the bride of Thirteen Curves: a presumably plastic skeleton covered with fabric and clutching a bouquet of withered flowers, hung between two maple trees near the driveway of area resident David D'Ambrosio, who lives just off Cedarvale Road on Balcomb Mill Circle. The fairly artfully constructed and mounted "bride" certainly could be construed as a ghost in dim light, especially if fog obscured the view.

Onondaga Historical Association curator of history Dennis Conners added his own doubts to the stories of the cursed spirits. "There's a series of curves, and the woods are quite close to the road, so you have a situation where automobile headlights are constantly driving down the road, scanning and sweeping through the forest along the edge of the road," he told a blogger on Tumblr. "So it's the perfect setting to have the tale of a bride who got killed on her wedding night appearing along that road."

These revelations, however, seem not to have tarnished the reputation of the tragic ghost one fantastical iota.

23

PHANTOM SHIPS
ON THE HUDSON

When New York was young—so young, in fact, that the early settlers called it New Netherlands—few things could stir the souls of the colonists like the arrival of a ship. Spotting a ship in the distance meant that casks and crates filled with supplies from across the ocean, far down the coast, or the islands of the East Indies could be on their way. Sails and masts on the horizon sent soldiers from forts to alert neighbors, who in turn ran from one house to the next, calling, "A ship! A ship!" and sending the message far and wide to the next settlement up the Hudson River. Such a day promised good fortune and news of family and home for all.

Unless, of course, the ship proved to be a phantom, a specter with a motionless crew making silent progress for no clear reason at all.

The great historian and storyteller Washington Irving wrote of just such a ship in his book *Bracebridge Hall*, a collection of essays and stories published in 1822. He tells of a ship appearing off the coast of New Netherlands after a storm—the kind of storm that meteorologists and water authorities now call a "hundred-year storm," or a gale that comes along only once in a century. The storm came right around the time of the summer solstice in June, and once the clouds finally broke and the sun emerged to make "the broad bosom of the bay to gleam like a sea of molten gold," the soldiers at Fort Amsterdam on the Manhattoes harbor (now Battery Park in Manhattan) sent word throughout the settlements: they had sighted a ship in the bay.

The townspeople throughout the area crowded to the battery, each offering their own speculation about which ship this might be, as no one had expected a ship at that particular time of the season. Soon the vessel became clear to the naked eye: "She was a stout, round Dutch-built vessel, with high bow and poop, and bearing Dutch colors. The evening sun gilded her bellying canvas, as she came riding over the long waving billows."

A Dutch ship! Surely it must bring much-needed supplies from Holland, the country all these settlers had left behind years ago.

Something simply was not right with this ship, however. One of the sentinels reported that he had not seen the ship until it had already reached the center of the bay, when it had suddenly popped into view, "just as if she had come out of the bosom of the black thunder-cloud." Ships normally could be seen once they had broken the horizon, getting larger as they approached. This one did not behave like a normal ship.

How could it be anything but a ship? The settlers shrugged off this description and waited for the vessel to come closer. Soldiers at the fort began hailing the ship, but the crew, now visible as they stood on the deck, made no reply at all. In fact, they stood silent and motionless as the ship passed the fort.

Still attempting to get the captain's attention, the soldiers loaded a gun and fired it across the ship's bow. As if no shot had been fired, the ship continued to glide northward up the Hudson River, making no acknowledgment of the fort, the settlers, or the gunfire.

Irving reports that a seaman named Hans Van Pelt then ordered his boat and began rowing toward the ship, making to board her once he pulled up alongside her. "[B]ut after rowing two or three hours, he returned without success. Sometimes he would get within one or two hundred yards of her, and then, in a twinkling, she would be half a mile off. . . . He got near enough to see the crew; who were all dressed in the Dutch style, the officers in doublets and high hats and feathers; not a word was spoken by any one on board; they stood as motionless as so many statues, and the ship seemed as if left to her own government."

The ship continued on its way upriver until it faded from view, without ever once making a sign that would suggest reason or life on board.

What on earth was this?

The governor of the settlements along the Hudson River began to fear that this might be an enemy ship, carefully disguised as a Dutch ship to allow a swift invasion and destruction of the new colonies. He sent messengers north in sloops to the other settlements, but they all came back with the same story: The ship passed through silently, making no sign that its crew saw or cared to see the people signaling from the riverbanks. At no point did it vary its course to make any port. The captains of these vessels reported their own sightings of the phantom ship, sometimes spotting her in a flash of lightning on an otherwise dark night, and sometimes as a silhouette on a moonlit night as the silent vessel perused the highlands. When the sloop captains changed their own course to pursue the ship, however, it disappeared in an instant. Moments later, they would catch another glimpse of her, back in the area from which they had just come.

Speculation ran rampant along the river's banks. There were tales already circulating that Hendrick Hudson, the first explorer to navigate this river, haunted the Catskill Mountains with his ship's crew; perhaps he captained this ghostly ship. Over time, as the ship continued to appear and disappear along the Hudson as far north as the Tappan Sea and all the way south to Hoboken (in what would become New Jersey), government officials in the area began to believe that a sighting was a portent of the invasion by England to come. Once the Redcoats did arrive and the Dutch provinces became the property of the British crown, sightings of the phantom ship came to an end, turning endless speculation into fact—as much as there can be facts about a ghost ship— that the ship's eternal voyage warned of the trouble to come.

"Since that time, we have no authentic accounts of her," Irving wrote, "though it is said she still haunts the highlands and cruises about Point-no-point. People who live along the river, insist that they sometimes see her in summer moonlight; and that in a deep still midnight, they have heard the chant of her crew, as if heaving the lead; but sights and sounds are so deceptive along the mountainous shores, and about the wide bays and long reaches of this great river, that I confess I have very strong doubts upon the subject."

THE CURSE OF THE ETERNAL VOYAGE

Tales of phantom ships—ships with no living crew or passengers on-board—have appeared in history since the early 1700s, and some even pop up in ancient, localized mythologies around the world. Most of these stories begin as accounts of a real shipwreck in stormy seas, though some tell tales of deliberate wrecks perpetrated by mutinous crewmembers, a fire on board that caused a wooden ship to sink, or an encounter with an unexpectedly rocky coastline that caused fatal damage to a ship's hull. In all cases, the ship went down with its crew aboard . . . and the crew continues to man the ship, either standing motionless on deck in full uniform or stripped down to skeletons, rowing madly into eternity.

"I have not come across any phantom steamers—only sailing craft," reported Ralph deS. Childs, writing in 1949 for the *New York Folklore Quarterly*. "There are no reports of ghosts of the *Titanic*, the *Antinoe*, the *Atlantique*, the *Vestris*, or the *Morro Castle*. Well-established ghosts of sailing ships are still being seen, however, and many of them are ghosts of ships that have met disaster."

Childs documented fifteen phantom ships north and east of New York, discovering only two that actually appear in the waters of New York State. One is the Dutch ship Washington Irving chronicled, while the other suffers from an eternal inability to arrive in port.

The rowing vessel owned by Rambout Van Dam of Spuyten Duyvil (Spiting Devil), New York, cannot be seen by people standing on shore, but residents and visitors around the Tappan Zee area can hear a low sound, a scraping of wood against oarlocks, that lets them know that the crew of this ship continues to work through the night to make port. "Some might have supposed that a boat was rowed along unseen under the deep shadows on the opposite shore," Irving writes in his book, *Wolfert's Roost*, "but the ancient traditionists of the neighborhood knew better."

The neighbors told the tale of Van Dam's dalliance of a Saturday night, when he rowed alone across the Tappan Sea (presumably the bay where the Tappan Zee Bridge stands now) to go to a quilting party in a town on the western shore. "Here he danced and drunk until midnight when he entered his boat to return home," Irving wrote. "He was warned that he was on the verge of Sunday morning, but he pulled off nevertheless, swearing that he would not land until he reached Spiting Devil if it took him a month of Sundays."

Van Dam never reached Spiting Devil, and no one ever saw him again. In the silence of a spring evening, however, the settlers could hear his oars squealing in the oarlocks as he labored to reach the dock on the eastern shore and to arrive home at last.

Traffic may prevent you from hearing Van Dam's oars today, but if you visit in the wee hours of the morning when the noise of cars racing across the bridge briefly subsides, you may still catch the sounds of a stroke or two of his oars.

24

THE CURSED GHOST OF ALICE VAN DER VEER

In the early days of New York, when the Dutch settled along the Hudson and Mohawk Rivers and the English had not yet ventured into the farther reaches of the territory, there lived a man named Jan Van der Veer and his beautiful seventeen-year-old daughter, Alice. Some who tell this story place it at around 1672.

Accounts of this time say that Van der Veer settled in what is now Rotterdam Junction in Schenectady, near the site of Union College. Known for his quick temper and his generally volatile personality, the old curmudgeon did not attract friends—in fact, some said he was a murderer who had run to the New World to escape certain imprisonment. Reclusive and possessive of his daughter, Van der Veer hated to see any suitor vying for Alice's attentions. He chased them off, one by one, with threatening words and displays of his rifle, and no one doubted that he would be willing to use it.

The other settlers would have been just as happy to leave the old man in peace, but Alice attracted many a young man to Van der Veer's home and farmlands. She had the good sense to take no interest in them, however, so her father's promises of violence and worse did not much bother her. She spent her days taking care of her father's home and helping with whatever she could on his substantial farm.

"Can we imagine a portrait of young Alice?" suggests writer B. A. Nilsson of Glen, New York, in retelling the story on his Blogspot blog, *Words and Music.* "She wears the Dutch costume of her day, lovely brown hair tucked into the traditional stern cap, eyes modestly lowered as she passes the men of the settlement. But she has a rebellious spirit, born of enduring her father's harshness. For reasons that would gladden only the staunchest Calvinist, this would be her undoing."

One day, one of the suitors managed to sneak past her father and caught Alice's eye. Against her better judgment, she spoke to this young man, a grocer from Schenectady who was popular with the townspeople, and by the end of their conversation, she said she would not object to him visiting again. He risked his life over and over again to speak to Alice, eventually winning her heart. Alice fell hopelessly in love with her suitor, and agreed to meet him repeatedly for twilight walks along the Mohawk River out of her father's sight.

On a moonlit summer night, Van der Veer caught on to his daughter's lengthy disappearances and followed her as she went to meet her new love, trailing her to the area that is now the site of Lock Eight in Scotia. Historian Duane Featherstonaugh admirably described what happened next in a lecture he gave at the Schenectady County Historical Society in 1943 (in his version, the family's last name is Van Verveer):

> A rage swept the cunning Van Verveer. He fingered the rifle he carried as he carefully stalked the young couple. Unaware that they were being followed, the boy and girl walked down the south bank of the Mohawk until they came to the present site of the American Locomotive Company. There they sat down to rest and to pledge their love. Van Verveer crept up behind them. He leveled his rifle. A single shot shattered the soft stillness of summer and the boy slumped forward, dead.

Alice screamed, but Van der Veer had no time for histrionics. Knowing that the loud crack of his weapon firing and Alice's cries would attract neighbors and townspeople, he grabbed her arm and pulled her away, and the two fled into the woods.

Sure enough, the townspeople came running. They discovered the body of the young man with the bloody, fatal wound, and they took off after Van der Veer and his lovely daughter. It didn't take long to overtake the elderly man and yank his shotgun from his hands. They carried him to a grove of trees, erected a stake, tied him to it, and burned him to death.

As Van der Veer burned, some of the townspeople decided that Alice was every bit as guilty as her father, as she had lured the young man into a dangerous situation with her feminine wiles. Mob mentality took over, and the crowd whipped themselves up into believing that Alice had concocted the entire plan herself, to get rid of a father they all knew was a loathsome and terrifying creature.

As the clocks ticked on toward midnight, a section of the mob set out to find Alice and bring her to justice as well.

Poor Alice, already shaking with fear and grief and consumed with guilt over the deaths of her lover and her father, had run as far as she could until her feet were bloody. When she stumbled into the creek known as Hans Grott Kill, a waterway hidden from view by the night, the townspeople trapped her there, dragged her out of the water, and carried her off for their brand of justice. Some accounts say they tied her to a stake next to her smoldering father, lit the tinder below, and set her aflame as well. Others say that the mob did not bother to bring her all the way back to the execution ground, and lynched her then and there from a tree on the banks of Hans Grott Kill.

Either way, Alice died a horrifying death as the price of her love.

CURSED TO WAIT FOREVER

Nearly 350 years have passed since this gruesome murder and its vigilante justice, but to this day, on nights with a full moon, the ghost of Alice Van der Veer returns to the Union College campus and wanders through Jackson's Garden, hoping to find the ghost of her lover.

Consumed with pain, guilt, and a passion that can never be fully requited, Alice remains cursed by her grisly death and her separation from the only man she ever loved. The stories never suggest that she seeks revenge; instead, she walks the garden the way she once walked along the river with her young man, hoping beyond hope that he might return to this special place as well.

Those who have watched for her say that Alice's ghost appears around 9:00 p.m. at Rotterdam Junction, strolls along the bank of the Mohawk River as if she walks with her lover, and then moves on to Union Street until she reaches Jackson's Garden.

"There are those who say that on many summer nights, but especially on the night of the first full moon in July, the whole tragic climax of the story is repeated on the Union College campus," wrote James G. Shaw Jr. in the *New York Folklore Quarterly* in May 1946. "And some people have reported seeing the ghost of a young girl, a great red bruise on her neck, wandering the banks of the Mohawk looking and crying in vain for her lover."

Many a Union College student has a story of an Alice sighting, the feeling of a presence, or a strange occurrence that they eagerly attribute to her. Some report a sudden gust of powerful wind and a chill in the otherwise balmy air when she comes to the garden.

Every story, however, has a matching, equally vehement denial. Wayne Somers, author of the *Encyclopedia of Union College History*, finds the whole tale more deniable than plausible. "There is no evidence that an Alice Van der Veer ever existed, or that any such incident ever occurred in Schenectady," he noted. "Nor is it clear that anyone ever seriously claimed to see the ghost; the story is probably more correctly classified as modern fiction than as legitimate folklore."

Perhaps . . . and perhaps not. On July 14, 2003, on the first full moon of summer, Union College hosted a national fundraising conference with at least 150 annual fund officers in attendance. Most were housed in Davidson Hall, one of the campus residence halls—at least, they were until a campus-wide power failure made staying there much less comfortable. When the power could not be restored in the morning, conference organizers determined that the guests would be moved to a hotel.

In the October 31, 2003, issue of the college's newsletter, the *Chronicle*, a campus safety officer suggested that, given the timing, the outage might just have been the work of the ghost of Alice Van der Veer. The young lady's ghost may have developed some additional powers over the ensuing 331 years.

25

POLITICS AND
PAINTED POULTRY

For the last chapter in this collection of tales, let's turn to another realm of folkloric, historic, and inexplicable behavior on which we have not yet touched in this volume. We've learned about suspected curses in the arts, sports, religion, agriculture, and law, so it must be time to look at politics.

On December 30, 2013, Gwen Goodwin, a Democratic candidate for New York City Council—a candidate who had lost the primary by twenty-six points the previous September—filed a million-dollar lawsuit against one of her five opponents: the frontrunner for speaker of the City Council, Melissa Mark-Viverito. Goodwin claimed that Mark-Viverito intentionally inflicted "emotional distress" by putting a Caribbean hex on her while they were running for the same seat on City Council.

That's right, this happened in 2014.

How did Mark-Viverito hex Goodwin? She perpetrated this hoax—er, *hex*—by ordering the painting of a mural on the building in which Goodwin lived.

You see, Mark-Viverito, who was born in Puerto Rico, took the leadership role in an urban art campaign called *Los Muros Hablan*, or "The Walls Speak." The campaign began in 2013 and celebrates Latino culture, using colorful murals painted on buildings throughout the five boroughs to draw positive attention to the vibrancy of Latino religious and cultural symbols. One of the people Mark-Viverito worked with to place these murals throughout New York happened to be Goodwin's landlord, of Eastside Managers' Associates.

When the spectacular head of a rooster—sporting a multicolored crest and bright purple wattles—appeared five stories tall on Goodwin's building on East 100th Street, the Democratic hopeful said that all kinds of shenanigans began in her life. Goodwin's apartment is on the sixth floor, and the rooster appears just below her window.

The lawsuit, *Gwen Goodwin v. Melissa Mark-Viverito and Eastside Managers' Associates*, alleges that "the conduct of the Defendants has been extreme and outrageous, intentionally calculated to cause, and causing, the infliction of emotional distress, from which the Plaintiff has suffered." It goes on to explain, "The mural depicted a decapitated and wooden-sword-stabbed bird of prey, on information and belief, and according to neighbors of Puerto Rican and other backgrounds, in the Caribbean culture, this constituted a curse and a death threat."

The lawsuit also takes the landlord to task for volunteering its property for the mural: "The Plaintiff was and is Landlord EMA's rent-stabilized tenant who has defeated said landlord in many frivolous and vexatious court cases perpetrated against the Plaintiff by said Landlord . . . in addition to a years-long series of other acts of spite, nastiness, mischief and harassment by Defendant EMA, the Landlord against the Plaintiff."

In the lawsuit, Goodwin calls the mural "frightening, scary, and perceived evil," and notes that it "would not be a capital improvement to the building . . . the graffiti-like mural actually lowers the property value and put a downward pressure on prospective rents of apartments."

She brought up the scariness again when she was interviewed by the media. "This intimated [*sic*] me and caused me fear," she told the *New York Post*. "I'm a Christian. I don't believe outside my religion, but strange things were happening."

Among the odd things Goodwin experienced were the sudden appearance of a blood clot in her foot and a close friend who began "acting crazy" after the mural appeared. Goodwin did not go so far as to blame the mural for her loss of the primary, however.

Her sources for the claims of malevolence were people in the neighborhood who had told her that the mural had voodoo-like properties. "According to neighbors of Puerto Rican and other backgrounds, in the Caribbean culture, this constituted a curse and a death threat, as a swastika or a noose would symbolize typically to many Jews or African-Americans," the lawsuit filed in Manhattan Supreme Court alleges.

There seemed no question that the lawsuit had more to do with Mark-Viverito's position as frontrunner to become speaker of the New York City Council than any real harm the mural may have done to Goodwin. In fact, the plaintiff said as much: "I really felt that people needed to understand who they were giving power to as the next most powerful person behind the mayor of New York City," Goodwin told the *New York Post.*

A CASE OF SANTERIA

Goodwin's allegations do have some basis in fact: The symbol of a rooster does have a religious connotation. One of the many religions with island origins is Santeria, a religion that many people of the Caribbean practice right along with Catholicism, making it a *syncretic* religion. This means that it can be blended into another religion even though the belief systems may seem contrary to one another on the surface.

Santeria brings together the beliefs of Yoruba mythology from Nigeria and Native American traditions. It promotes a connection between the human and natural world and a relationship with the spiritual and the divine, teaching people to live in harmony with these forces and with one another.

People who practice Santeria worship specific saints, based on parallels drawn between the Catholic saints and the Santeria *orishas,* or deities. This provided a fairly clever way for slaves brought from Africa to continue to practice their religion, even though their Western masters forbade them to do so. By determining which of their deities matched those of Christianity, they could practice Santeria while appearing to practice Catholicism.

Santeria rituals often involve sacred drumming, dancing, wearing and carrying symbols of the religion, and a complex series of initiation rites that lead each person to find which of the *orishas* they will worship. The hierarchy of deities is much too complicated to go into here, but one of them is indeed represented by the figure of a rooster.

Osun (also known as Ozun) is part of the top level of the hierarchy, a protector of the head of Santeria practitioners, and his primary purpose is to alert people to danger, "to let us know when there's a serious threat to our physical or spiritual well-being," according to AboutSanteria.com. "He's a symbol of good health and stability in life. In the home, Osun stands on guard and never sleeps. Santeros keep him on a high shelf or on top of a bookcase, somewhere that allows him to see what goes on in the house."

Perhaps his watchful eye on the fifth floor of an apartment building in East Harlem provides just this kind of protection.

So is Santeria voodoo? No—and, for that matter, voodoo isn't even voodoo; at least, it's not the notion of voodoo popularized by television and movies. Vodou, the religion practiced in Haiti, has its own pantheon of deities, called *lwa,* who are often called through prayer using ornate drawings laid out on the ground or on tables. This may be why some confused the mural on Goodwin's apartment building with the kinds of murals used in Haitian Vodou practices.

Perhaps Goodwin's neighbors also were confused by the practice of hoodoo, a form of folk magic used in the southern United States, that employs the techniques practiced in the Congo and other parts of the African continent. Hoodoo is not part of a larger religious practice; it involves casting spells, sometimes while chanting psalms or passages from the Bible, but without any deeper connection to religion. (That's why these practitioners are often simply called conjurers.)

"In our religion, we sometimes will sacrifice a rooster to a specific orisha like Elegua to 'feed' the orisha," said Cynthia Duncan, PhD, a practitioner of Santeria who writes the Santeria.com website. Dr. Duncan and I corresponded directly via email. "This is to bring good luck, open the doors, ask for help with a problem. Usually the rooster will be eaten afterwards. It's not scary and not something to fear; it is not used to do harm to people or curse them. Just the opposite. We don't put curses on people or throw witchcraft at them because any harm we do to others comes back to us."

It's likely that the rooster on Goodwin's building is nothing more than an interesting mural, Dr. Duncan suggested. "Certainly no one who is initiated in the religion would paint a rooster on a building; that makes no sense."

"For centuries, the African Traditional Religions (ATRs) have been the victim of racism and colonial stereotypes," wrote the Reverend Dr. Ekun Dayo Oni Shango on the website SanteriaChurch.org. "This was an institutionalized way of dehumanizing the African people by labeling their religious practices as barbaric or demonic. This changed society's perception of black people into animals or subhuman, in order to justify the slave trade and the brutal treatment of African people. . . . It is common to portray these religions as nothing more than harmful spell casters focusing on zombifying people, using voodoo dolls to harm people, or engaging in cannibalism or pacts with the devil. Satan does not exist in Santeria. Satan is not worshipped in the ATRs."

THE RESPONSE

"Darn! My little secret revealed!" Mark-Viverito tweeted on January 4, 2014, in response to a tweet from @SeamusCampbell, asking if she was "a voodoo temptress." She finished her tweet with #cant makethisup.

A few minutes later, Mark-Viverito tweeted again. "Gracias #ny post for putting a smile on my face this morning! #LaBrujaDelBarrio."

The official response was more pointed. "These desperate and ridiculous allegations by a failed political opponent of Melissa are false, absurd and a waste of the court's precious time," Mark-Viverito's official spokesperson, Eric Koch, told the media on the day the lawsuit was announced.

Organizations representing the Latino population of New York City and beyond came to Mark-Viverito's defense as well. "Both the *New York Post* and the *Daily News* owe not only Melissa Mark-Viverito, but the whole Puerto Rican and Caribbean population of this city an apology for this disgusting stereotyping and partisan political reporting," said Angelo Falcon, founder of the National Institute for Latino Policy.

The website Melissawatch.com took the opposite view. "Melissa Mark-Viverito is named as a defendant in a law suit charging she engaged in and instigated unlawful, vicious and wrongful acts, bordering on the criminal activity, and crossing a line to extend political campaigning into psychological warfare," a news release on the site read on January 2, 2014. "Its sole, conceivable purpose was a spiteful, hostile, mischievous assault, counter to the spirit in which even heated arguments are held in elections. . . . The mural had a likelihood of setting back campaign momentum, and may have been instrumental in wrongfully shaping the election result, even stealing the election, which would be irremedial damage . . . not only to Gwen Goodwin, but to all challenger candidates, the community and democracy itself."

That's some chicken.

THE UPSHOT

Despite all the vitriol over this case and the fervor with which Goodwin filed her lawsuit, nothing actually came of it in court. A Notice of Discontinuance was filed in the Supreme Court of the State of New York on May 7, 2014. The media took no notice.

In this tale, as with every story in this book, I simply report the facts as they were available to discover. This modern-day yarn of politics and painted poultry needed not a word of embellishment; the facts are too much fun all by themselves.

SOURCES

1. ANCIENT, UNSPORTSMANLIKE SOULS

Carlozo, Lou. "From Bad to Curse: The Real Reason The Cubs are 0-For-Wrigley." ChicagoSide, April 3, 2012. Accessed January 15, 2015. http://chicagosidesports.com/from-bad-to-curse-the-real-reason-the-cubs-are-0-for-wrigley.

Conklin, Mike. "Urban archaeologists dig into our past." *Chicago Tribune*, September 4, 2002. Accessed January 15, 2015. http://articles.chicagotribune.com/2002-09-04/features/0209040022_1_burial-ground-digging-archeologists.

Lowinger, Aaron. "The Bills Curse." *Buffalo Spree*, June 20, 2012. Accessed January 15, 2015. http://www.buffalospree.com/Buffalo-Spree/June-2012/The-Bills-Curse.

Lynch, Jason. "Amityville Ghosts: 30 Years Later." *People* magazine, April 18, 2005. Accessed January 15, 2015. http://www.people.com/people/article/0,,20147397,00.html.

Osuna, Ric. "Revealing The Facts." The Amityville Murders: The Official Website for the Amityville Murders. Accessed January 15, 2015. http://www.amityvillemurders.com/facts.html.

Parker, Arthur C. "The Archeological History of New York, Part 2." *New York State Museum Bulletin*, 1920, 235/236, page 554. Accessed January 15, 2015 at New York State Library website, Document ID: 65709. http://128.121.13.244/awweb/main.jsp?flag=browse&smd=1&awdid=1.

Rosen, Lawrence. "The Excavation of American Indian Burial Sites: A Problem in Law and Professional Responsibility." *American Anthropology* 82, no. 1 (March 1980): 5–27. Accessed January 16,

2015. http://users.clas.ufl.edu/krigbaum/proseminar/Ethics%20
March%207/Ethics%20(assigned%20readings)/descendant%20
communities/Nagpra/1980,%20Rosen,%20The%20excavation%20
of%20american%20indian%20burial%20sites.pdf.

Tucker, Libby. "Spectral Indians, Desecrated Burial Grounds." *Voices: The Journal of New York Folklore* 31 (Spring–Summer 2005). Accessed January 11, 2015. http://www.nyfolklore.org/pubs/voic31-1-2/spectral.html.

U.S. Government. Native American Graves Protection and Repatriation Act (1990). Accessed January 11, 2015. http://www.cr.nps.gov/local-law/FHPL_NAGPRA.pdf.

Windfield, Mason, and Michael Bastine. *Iroquois Supernatural: Talking Animals and Medicine People*. Rochester, VT: Bear & Company, 2011.

2. THE INDIAN PRINCESS OF LAKE RONKONKOMA

Eyewitness News. "Man Drowns Fetching Boat in Lake Ronkonkoma." WABC-TV New York. Accessed January 30, 2015. http://7online.com/archive/8712246.

Igneri, Dr. David S. *Lake Ronkonkoma in History and Legend, the Princess, Curse, and Other Stories: A Lifeguard's View*. Bloomington, IN: AuthorHouse, 2013.

Ruud, Candice, and Deborah S. Morris. "Body of Missing Kayaker Kevin Conley Recovered from Lake Ronkonkoma." *Newsday*, August 24, 2014. Accessed January 30, 2015. http://www.newsday.com/long-island/suffolk/kevin-conley-s-body-recovered-from-lake-ronkonkoma-cops-say-1.9134067.

The Suburban Fire Marshal. "Drowning in Lake Ronkonkoma." Accessed January 30, 2015. http://www.suburbanfiremarshal.org/news-feed/drowning-in-lake-ronkonkoma-2.html.

Unattributed. "Myths of Lake Ronkonkoma: The Bottomless Theory." Accessed via the Internet Archive Wayback Machine, January 15–22, 2015. http://wotan.liu.edu/~esenig/bottomlesstheory.html.

3. THE TRUTH ABOUT SHAKESPEARE'S SCOTTISH PLAY

"Astor Place Riot." Wikipedia. Accessed November 16, 2014. http://en.wikipedia.org/wiki/Astor_Place_Riot.

Cliff, Nigel. *The Shakespeare Riots: Revenge, Drama and Death in Nineteenth-Century America.* New York: Random House, 2007.

Crystal. "The Curse, Legend, and Superstitions of Shakespeare's *Macbeth*." Ticketnetwork.com, April 23, 2013. Accessed November 16, 2014. http://www.ticketnetwork.com/blog/post/2013/04/23/the-curse-legend-and-superstitions-of-shakespeares-macbeth.aspx.

"The Curse of Macbeth." TheLoneConspirators.com. Accessed November 16, 2014. http://www.theloneconspirators.com/macb.htm.

Gordon, Tom. "National Theatre Sued for $20m after Macbeth Accident in New York." *Herald Scotland,* April 27, 2013. Accessed November 19, 2014. http://www.heraldscotland.com/arts-ents/stage/national-theatre-sued-for-20m-after-macbeth-accident-in-new-york.20923065.

"National Theatre Faces £1.4m Payout." *Herald Scotland,* April 27, 2014. Accessed November 19, 2014. http://www.heraldscotland.com/news/home-news/national-theatre-faces-14m-payout.24067853.

Schall, Thomas. "Episode 187: Tony, Tony, Tony!" Reduced Shakespeare Company podcast. Accessed November 19, 2014. http://www.reducedshakespeare.com/tag/tom-schall.

"The Scottish Play." Wikipedia. Accessed November 16, 2014. http://en.wikipedia.org/wiki/The_Scottish_Play.

Shakespeare, William. *The Tragedy of Macbeth*. The Annotated Shakespeare. New York: Greenwich House, Crown, 1978.

Straight Dope Scientific Advisory Board. "What's the Story on the Curse of *Macbeth*?" October 16, 2007. Accessed November 16, 2014. http://www.straightdope.com/columns/read/2267/whats-the-story-on-the-curse-of-em-macbeth-em.

Webster, Richard. *The Encyclopedia of Superstitions*. Woodbury, MN: Llewellyn, 2008.

4. THE CURSE OF MAMIE O'ROURKE

Fetter, Henry D. "The Curse of the Belmont Stakes." *The Atlantic*. June 7, 2014. Accessed February 1, 2015. http://www.theatlantic.com/entertainment/archive/2014/06/the-curse-of-the-belmont-stakes/372358.

Hinckley, David. "From 'The Sidewalks of New York . . .' Mamie O'Rourke, Chapter 236." *New York Daily News*, December 10, 2002. Accessed February 1, 2015. http://www.nydailynews.com/archives/news/sidewalks-new-york-mamie-o-rourke-chapter-236-article-1.511970.

Kellner, Jenny, New York Racing Association. Personal interview on February 4, 2015.

Liebman, Bennett. "Ending the Triple Crown Curse." *New York Times*, June 10, 2008. Accessed February 1, 2015. http://therail.blogs. nytimes.com/2008/06/10/ending-the-triple-crown-curse/?_r=0.

New York Times staff. "Composer Tells of Sidewalks Song." *New York Times*, June 28, 1924. Accessed February 1, 2015. http:// timesmachine.nytimes.com/timesmachine/1924/06/28/119040056 .html?pageNumber=7.

Roberts, Sam. "Belmont Park Hopes Old Song Will Break Triple Crown Drought." *New York Times*, May 28, 2014. Accessed February 1, 2015. http://www.nytimes.com/2014/05/29/nyregion/belmont-park -hopes-old-song-will-break-triple-crown-drought.html.

Scheinman, John. "Five Myths About the Triple Crown." *Washington Post*, May 30, 2014. Accessed February 1, 2015. http://www .washingtonpost.com/opinions/five-myths-about-the-triple -crown/2014/05/30/9b18f1b2-e69f-11e3-a86b-362fd5443d19_story .html.

5. THE LOST SOULS OF SENECA COUNTY

"The Asylum." *Paranormal State*, season 1, #116, episode 20, first airing on A&E February 25, 2008.

Doran, Robert E., MD. "History of Willard Asylum for the Insane and the Willard State Hospital." Accessed February 15, 2015. http:// www.asylumprojects.org/Willard.pdf.

"Willard State Hospital." Port City Paranormal, Wilmington, NC. Accessed February 15, 2015. http://www.portcityparanormal.com/ asylum5.html.

6. THE BLACK DOG OF THE GREAT LAKES

"The Black Dog of Lake Erie." Dark Destinations. Accessed February 9, 2015. http://darkdestination.livejournal.com/61413.html.

Boyle, Terry. *Haunted Ontario 3: Ghostly Historic Sites, Inns, and Miracles.* Toronto: Dundurn, 2014.

The Cabinet. "Lake Erie: The Black Dog of Lake Erie." Accessed February 2, 2015. http://www.thecabinet.com/darkdestinations/location.php?sub_id=dark_destinations&letter=l&location_id=lake_erie.

"Isaac G. Jenkins (Schooner), U100078, Sunk, 30 Nov. 1875." Maritime History of the Great Lakes. Accessed February 9, 2015. http://images.maritimehistoryofthegreatlakes.ca/58054/data.

McGovern, Una. *Chambers Dictionary of the Unexplained.* Edinburgh: Chambers, 2007.

7. THE RANGERS, THE STANLEY CUP, AND THE CURSE OF 1940

Anderson, Dave. "Sports of the Times; Do You Believe in Curses?" *New York Times,* June 12, 1994. Accessed February 10, 2015. http://www.nytimes.com/1994/06/12/sports/sports-of-the-times-do-you-believe-in-curses.html.

Cohen, Russ. *100 Things Rangers Fans Should Know & Do Before They Die.* Chicago: Triumph Books, 2014.

"Curse of 1940." Ice Hockey Wiki. Accessed February 10, 2015. http://icehockey.wikia.com/wiki/Curse_of_1940.

Long, Steven. "Brooklyn's NHL Curse." *New York Post,* August 13, 2011. Accessed February 10, 2015. http://nypost.com/2011/08/13/brooklyns-nhl-curse.

"New York Rangers." Wikipedia. Accessed February 13, 2015. http://en.wikipedia.org/wiki/New_York_Rangers#1967.E2.80.931993.

"Tradition." Rangerstown, the New York Rangers official website. Accessed February 13, 2015. http://rangers.nhl.com/club/page.htm?id=56153.

8. THE DEATH OF A PRESIDENT AND THE TEAMS THAT FAIL TO THRIVE

"Biblical Judgment, Settled Science: Complete, Unabridged Guide to the Curse of Doug Flutie." Cold, Hard Football Facts, December 23, 2013. Accessed February 18, 2015. http://www.coldhardfootballfacts.com/content/biblical-judgment-settled-science-complete-unabridged-guide-to-the-curse-doug-flutie/27698.

BuffaloCurse.com. Accessed February 17, 2015. http://www.buffalocurse.com.

Davenport, Gary. "Do Recent Bad Breaks Give Credence to 'Cursed' Buffalo Bills?" BleacherReport.com. Accessed February 17, 2015. http://bleacherreport.com/articles/2274961-do-recent-bad-breaks-give-credence-to-cursed-buffalo-bills.

"Freemasonry." Wikipedia. Accessed February 17, 2015. http://en.wikipedia.org/wiki/Freemasonry#Ritual_and_symbolism.

"The Pan-American Exposition." Theodore Roosevelt Inaugural National Historic Site. Accessed February 17, 2015. http://www.trsite .org/learn/the-pan-american-expo.

Sullivan, Mike. "The Curse of Billy Buffalo." TheKickIsGood.com. Accessed February 17, 2015. http://www.thekickisgood.com/the -curse-of-billy-buffalo.

"What Is Freemasonry?" Masonic Higher Education Bursary Fund, Grand Lodge of Alberta. Accessed February 17, 2015. http://www .mhebf.com/freemasonry.html.

9. GUSTAV MAHLER AND THE CURSE OF THE NINTH SYMPHONY

"Classical Composer Superstitions: Curse of the Ninth." CMuse. Accessed February 21, 2015. http://www.cmuse.org/classical-composer-superstitions-curse-of-the-ninth.

"Gustav Mahler." Wikipedia. Accessed February 20, 2015. http://en .wikipedia.org/wiki/Gustav_Mahler.

Jok, Michael. "The Curse of the Ninth Symphony." CBC Music. Accessed February 21, 2015. http://music.cbc.ca/#!/blogs/2012/2/ The-Curse-of-the-Ninth-Symphony.

Lefevre, Peter. "Composers and the Curse of the Ninth Symphony." CSO Sounds and Stories, Chicago Symphony Orchestra. Accessed February 21, 2015. http://csosoundsandstories.org/composers-and-the-curse-of-the-ninth-symphony.

"List of Symphony Composers." Wikipedia. Accessed February 20, 2015. http://en.wikipedia.org/wiki/List_of_symphony_composers.

10. DEVIL'S HOLE: THE CAVE OF THE EVIL SPIRIT

"Devil's Hole and the Devil's Hole Massacre." Niagara Falls Thunder Alley. Accessed February 22, 2015. www.niagarafrontier.com/devilhole.html.

Kostoff, Bob. "Review: Devil's Hole Massacre Topic of Fresh, Interesting Study." *Niagara Falls Reporter,* January 18, 2005. Accessed March 24, 2015. http://www.niagarafallsreporter.com/kostoff78.html.

"René-Robert Cavilier, Sieur de La Salle." Wikipedia. Accessed February 22, 2015. http://en.wikipedia.org/wiki/René-Robert_Cavelier,_Sieur_de_La_Salle.

Williams, Edward T. "The Legend of Devil's Hole." *Williams' Scenic and Historic Niagara Falls.* 1925. Quoted at NiagaraFrontier.com. Accessed February 22, 2015. http://www.niagarafrontier.com/image/devilcavetablet.jpg.

11. THE HEX MURDER AT THE STONE ARCH BRIDGE

Conway, John. "Retrospect: A Halloween Ghost Story." Reposted on Facebook by Between the Lakes Group LLC, October 26, 2012. Accessed March 24, 2015. https://www.facebook.com/betweenthelakes/posts/210986809033630.

Crane, Caroline. *Murder and Mayhem in the Catskills.* The History Press, 2008. Accessed on Google Books, March 24, 2015. https://books.google.com/books?id=Xvwx5jOBnOAC&pg=PA33&lpg=PA33&dq=murder+at+Stone+Arch+Bridge&source=bl&ots=AMp_JAakPH&sig=P_Z5cDaS4AEBpKyJ4Ct35Tc06Qw&hl=en&sa=X&ei=tWYRV

e21FsavggTygoT4Bg&ved=0CFoQ6AEwCQ#v=onepage&q=murder
%20at%20Stone%20Arch%20Bridge&f=false.

"The Stone Arch Bridge." Sullivan County Historical Society,
November 3, 2011. Accessed March 24, 2015. http://www.sullivan
countyhistory.org/index.php?option=com_content&view=article
&id=458:the-stone-arch-bridge&catid=51:delaware&Itemid=80.

12. MURDER IN THE WELL:
HAMILTON, BURR, AND THE QUAKER CURSE

Biographical Directory of the United States Congress. Accessed
January 4, 2015. http://bioguide.congress.gov/biosearch/biosearch
.asp.

"Burr-Hamilton Duel." Wikipedia. Accessed January 4, 2015. http://
en.wikipedia.org/wiki/Burr-Hamilton_duel.

Carr, Nick. "At SoHo Eatery, A Historic Haunt." *Wall Street Journal*,
October 25, 2011. Accessed January 4, 2015. http://www.wsj.com/
articles/SB10001424052970204644504576651252000172140.

Collins, Paul. *Duel With the Devil: The True Story of How Alexander
Hamilton and Aaron Burr Teamed Up to Take on America's First Sensational
Murder Mystery*. New York: Crown (Kindle edition), 2013.

Huguenin, Charles A. "The Quaker's Curse in New York City's First
'Love Murder.'" *New York Folklore Quarterly* XVIII, no. 3 (Autumn 1962).

"Levi Weeks Trial: 1800—A Less Than Discreet Affair, Weeks Indicted
for Murder, A Two-Day Trial." Law Library—American Law and
Legal Information. Accessed January 4, 2015. http://law.jrank.org/
pages/2398/Levi-Weeks-Trial-1800-Less-than-Discreet-Affair.html.

Lewis, Fairweather. "A Curse." Posted May 22, 2010. Accessed January 4, 2015. https://fairweatherlewis.wordpress.com/2010/05/22/a-curse/.

13. THE POWER OF A MALEFICENT GEM

Fraser, Paul (Paul Fraser Collectibles). "The Famous and Infamous Jewellery Collection of Henry Philip Hope." Picollecta, August 2014. Accessed March 26, 2015. https://www.picollecta.com/p/the-famous-and-infamous-jewellery-collections-of-henry-philip-hope-1000507409.

"Hope Diamond." Wikipedia. Accessed March 26, 2015. http://en.wikipedia.org/wiki/Hope_Diamond.

"Hope Diamond Coming Here." *New York Times*, November 14, 1901. Accessed March 26, 2015. http://query.nytimes.com/mem/archive-free/pdf?res=9900E1DD173BE733A25757C1A9679D946097D6CF.

"Hope Diamond . . . Curses Debunked." *Treasures of the World.* PBS.org. Accessed March 26, 2015. http://www.pbs.org/treasuresoftheworld/a_nav/hope_nav/hnav_level_1/5_debunk_hopfrm.html.

"J. R. M'Lean's Son Buys Hope Diamond." *New York Times*, January 29, 1911. Accessed March 29, 2015. http://query.nytimes.com/gst/abstract.html?res=9C02E2D71731E233A2575AC2A9679C946096D6CF.

"M'Leans Didn't Know Hope Diamond Tale; Wealthy Couple Unaware that the Famous Gem Had Brought Misfortune to Its Owners." *New York Times*, March 12, 1911. Accessed March 29, 2015. http://query.nytimes.com/gst/abstract.html?res=9E0DE7D71331E233A25751C1A9659C946096D6CF.

"U.S. Inflation Calculator." http://www.in2013dollars.com/1911-dollars-in-2015?amount=300000.

Wise, Richard W. "Historical Timeline, The French Blue." Accessed March 26, 2015. http://thefrenchblue.com/timeline.htm#.

14. THE CURSE OF THE BLACK ORLOV

"The Black Orlov Joins Diamonds." Natural History Museum website, London, England, September 21, 2005. Accessed April 10, 2015. http://www.nhm.ac.uk/about-us/news/2005/sept/news_6429.html.

"Famous Color Diamonds: Black Orlov (Black)." Langerman Diamonds Encyclopedia. Accessed March 29, 2015. http://www.langerman-diamonds.com/encyclopedia/5-31/black-orlov-black.html.

Gruosi, Fawaz. *The Black Diamond*. Geneva: De Grisogono, 1995.

Harlow, George. *The Nature of Diamonds*. Cambridge: Cambridge University Press, 1997. Accessed on Amazon.com, March 29, 2015.

"Jeweler in Fatal Plunge." *New York Times*, April 7, 1932. Accessed March 29, 2015. http://query.nytimes.com/mem/archive-free/pdf?res=9C04EFDF173EE633A25754C0A9629C946394D6CF.

Jury, Louise. "Curse of the 'Eye of Brahma' Comes to London." *The Independent*, September 21, 2005, Home section, page 11.

Minton, Mark. "Tale of Curse Adds Luster to Black Diamond." *Arkansas Democrat-Gazette*, October 2, 2005, p. 3A.

"New Evil Gem Death." Associated Press, December 2, 1947.

Roskin, Gary, G.G., FGA. "Black Orlov Sells at Christie's." *JCK Magazine*, January 2007. Accessed April 10, 2015. http://www
.jckonline.com/article/291201-Black_Orlov_Sells_at_Christie_s.php.

Roy, Amit. "Irresistible Lure of a Curse." *The Telegraph*, September 23, 2005. Accessed April 10, 2015. http://www.telegraphindia.com/
1050923/asp/nation/story_5274336.asp.

Wahl Jewelers. "Cursed Diamonds: The Black Orlov." R. C. Wahl Jewelers, August 21, 2014. Accessed March 29, 2015. http://www
.wahljewelers.com/cursed-diamonds-the-black-orlov.

15. THE WIDOW'S CURSE ON HYDE HALL

"Ann Low Clarke." Geni.com. Accessed April 6, 2015. http://www
.geni.com/people/Ann-Low-Clarke/6000000015749969735.

Cooper, James Fenimore. *The Legends and Traditions of a Northern County*. New York: The Knickerbocker Press, G. P. Putnam's Sons, 1921.

"Cooper Family Papers, 1786–1947." Special Collections—Manuscript Finding Aids, New York State Historical Association and the Farmers Museum. Accessed April 6, 2015. http://library.nysha.org/
special_collections/wp/?page_id=92.

Cordery, Stacy A. "Mary Gale Carter Clarke's Troubled Romance." April 13, 2012. Accessed April 6, 2015. http://www.stacycordery
.com/juliette-gordon-low/mary-gale-carter-clarkes-troubled
-romance.

"George Hyde Clarke." Geni.com. Accessed April 6, 2015. http://
www.geni.com/people/George-Clarke/6000000015750328048.

"Guide to the George Hyde Clarke Family Papers, 1705–1937." Collection Number 2800, Division of Rare and Manuscript Collections, Cornell University Library. Accessed April 6, 2015. http://rmc.library.cornell.edu/EAD/htmldocs/RMM02800.html.

"Hyde Hall's Origins." Hyde Hall official site. Accessed March 31, 2015. http://hydehall.org/about/history.

Owens, Mitchell. "Hyde Hall." Beekman 1802. Accessed April 6, 2015. http://beekman1802.com/hyde-hall.

Smith, Larry. Personal interview, April 2, 2015.

16. THE CASTLE IN THE CATSKILLS

Arnold, Walter. "The Mason's Castle: Ghost of the American Renaissance." The Art of Abandonment, July 29, 2011. Accessed April 9, 2015. http://artofabandonment.com/2011/07/dundas-castle -ghost-of-the-american-renaissance.

Conway, John. "Mystery Still Shrouds Dundas Castle." *Times Herald-Record*, October 27, 1993. Accessed April 9, 2015. http://www .dupontcastle.com/castles/craig-e.htm.

"Mission Statement." The Most Worshipful Prince Hall Grand Lodge of New York. Accessed April 9, 2015. http://princehallny.org.

"Ravenloft Castle." Abandoned NY, August 31, 2012. Accessed April 9, 2015. http://www.abandonedny.com/2012/08/ravenloft-castle.html.

Sokolow, Jane. "Dundas Castle." Friends of Beaverkill Community. Accessed April 9, 2015. http://beaverkillfriends.org/Pages/ StoryV2Dundas.html.

White, W. A., and S. E. Jeliffe. *The Psychoanalytic Review* 3. Harvard University, 1916, digitized October 25, 2007. Accessed on Google Books, April 9, 2015. https://books.google.com/books?id= 1u8PAAAAYAAJ&dq=sanitorium+Flavis+Packer+Riverdale&source =gbs_navlinks_s.

17. BRINGING *MALOCCHIO* TO AMERICA

Buonanno, Michael. "Ethnicity, Nostalgia, Affirmation: The Rhetoric of Italian American Identity." *Voices: The Journal of New York Folklore* 37 (Fall–Winter 2011): 1. Accessed April 10, 2015. http://www .nyfolklore.org/pubs/voic37-3-4/ethnicity.html.

Charles, Michael A. "'I Think the Baby's Got *Malocchio*' (Evil Eye as Faith)." *New York Folklore Newsletter* 20, no. 1 (Spring/Summer 1999): 11.

Crawford, Peter. "*Malocchio*: Ever-Present, All-Seeing Eye." Girosole: Italy Travel Information. Accessed April 10, 2015. http://www .girosole.com/italy-travel-info/art-malocchio-evil-eye.html.

Dundes, Alan. *The Evil Eye: A Casebook*. Madison: University of Wisconsin Press, 1981. Accessed on Google Books. https://books .google.com/books?id=gUDnzAfDleEC&pg=PA161&lpg=PA161&dq =evil+eye+Italian+New+York+State&source=bl&ots=ADWk2r HUzn&sig=7nlBVnNnGU0LTMgaVBbqDlExEzs&hl=en&sa=X&ei =ZFcoVZ3TOIa7ggTexoKQBg&ved=0CDMQ6AEwAw#v=onepage &q=evil%20eye%20Italian%20New%20York%20State&f=false.

Fabio, Michelle. "*Malocchio*: Conquering the Italian Evil Eye One Plastic Red Horn at a Time." Bleeding Espresso, January 19, 2007. Accessed April 10, 2015. http://bleedingespresso.com/2007/01/ conquering-evil-one-plastic-red-horn-at-a-time.html.

Hartman, Peter, and Karyl McIntosh. "Evil Eye Beliefs Collected in Utica, New York." *New York Folklore Quarterly* 4, nos. 1–4 (Summer 1978): 61–69.

King James Bible. Accessed April 15, 2015. http://www.kingjames bibleonline.org.

Ricci-Canham, Hollis, and Andrew Canham. *Legendary Locals of Orleans County, New York.* Charleston, SC: Arcadia, 2012.

18. THE SCANDALOUS CASE OF THE WITCH OF EASTHAMPTON

Drake, Samuel G. *Annals of Witchcraft in New England and Elsewhere in the United States.* Salem, NH: Ayer, 2003.

"Elizabeth Garlick: Notable Women Ancestors." Rootsweb. Accessed April 11, 2015. http://www.rootsweb.ancestry.com/~nwa/garlick.html.

Hanc, John. "Before Salem, There Was the Not-So-Wicked Witch of the Hamptons." Smithsonian.com: Exploring the American Experience, October 25, 2012. Accessed April 11, 2015. http://www.smithsonianmag.com/history/before-salem-there-was-the-not-so-wicked-witch-of-the-hamptons-95603019/?all.

Rattiner, Dan. "Goody Garlick: The True Story of the Woman Tried for Witchcraft in East Hampton." Dan's Papers, November 1, 2012. Accessed April 11, 2015. http://www.danspapers.com/2012/11/goody-garlick-the-true-story-of-the-woman-tried-for-witchcraft-in-east-hampton.

"Witches of Long Island." Brooklyn Genealogy Information Page. Accessed April 11, 2015. http://bklyn-genealogy-info.stevemorse. org/LI/WitchesofLongIsland.html.

19. "WICKED AND DETESTABLE ARTS" IN SEATALLCOTT

Burr, George Lincoln, ed. "Witchcraft in New York: The Cases of Hall and Harrison." *Narratives of Witchcraft Cases 1648–1706*. New York: C. Scribner's Sons, 1914. Accessed April 15, 2015. https://history .hanover.edu/texts/nyhah.html.

Howe, Katherine, ed. *The Penguin Book of Witches*. New York: Penguin, 2014. Accessed on Google Books, April 15, 2015. https://books .google.com/books?id=_rWQAwAAQBAJ&pg=PT50&lpg=PT50&dq= George+Wood+Ann+Rogers&source=bl&ots=8TQNMI-GQM&sig =HlaqG29l8fdqQSJ_tKozZ8b9s3E&hl=en&sa=X&ei=vKQuVc-w FMXFgwTB0IDwCw&ved=0CCcQ6AEwAg#v=onepage&q=George %20Wood%20Ann%20Rogers&f=false.

V'Kanty, Edward. *Testament: The Trial*. Ethereal Visions Press, Google Play ebook, 2015.

20. THE KNICKS, THE RED BULLS, AND THE WORST LUCK IN SPORTS

Beers, Anthony. "The Ewing Curse." *State Times*, February 5, 2014. Accessed April 11, 2015. http://thestatetimes.com/2014/02/05/ the-ewing-curse.

Heneage, Kristan. "Has the Curse of Caricola Reared Its Head For New York Bulls?" *World Soccer Talk*, November 6, 2013. Accessed April 12, 2015. http://worldsoccertalk.com/2013/11/06/has-the -curse-of-caricola-reared-its-head-for-new-york-red-bulls.

Major League Soccer. "The Curse of Caricola: *MLS Insider* Episode 15." October 26, 2013. Accessed April 11–12, 2015. https://www.youtube .com/watch?v=BFTjjLQs65o.

MetroFanatic. "Ten Years Ago: The Curse of Caricola." March 5, 2006. Accessed April 12, 2015. http://metrofanatic.com/story.jsp?ID=3276.

21. THE FARMER, THE BEGGAR, AND THE PEACH ORCHARD

"Cornell Gardening Resources: Growing Stone Fruits in New York." Cornell University Ecogardening Factsheet #12, Winter 1994. Accessed April 12, 2015. http://www.gardening.cornell.edu/ factsheets/ecogardening/growstone.html.

Sutton, Mayte E. "The Cursed Peach Orchard." *New York Folklore Quarterly* XVII, no. 4 (Winter 1961): 293.

22. THE LEGEND OF THIRTEEN CURVES

"The Bloody Bride of 13 Curves Road." Weird U.S. Accessed April 12, 2015. http://www.weirdus.com/states/new_york/road_less_traveled/ bloody_bride_of_13_curves/index.php.

Contrapunctusviii. "13 Curves." https://www.tumblr.com/ search/13%20curves.

Elzo, Eric. "Top 5 Urban Legends of Central New York." Syracuse.com, July 26, 2012. Accessed April 12, 2015. http://www.syracuse.com/news/index.ssf/2012/07/top_5_urban_legends_of_central.html.

Pierce, Frederic. "Fifth Stop: Thirteen Curves." Syracuse.com, November 1, 2007. Accessed April 12, 2015. http://blog.syracuse.com/strangecny/2007/11/fifth_stop_thirteen_curves.html.

Pierce, Frederic. "The Bride of 13 Curves Unveiled!!!!" Syracuse.com, November 2, 2007. Accessed April 12, 2015. http://blog.syracuse.com/strangecny/2007/11/the_bride_of_13_curves_unveile.html.

23. PHANTOM SHIPS ON THE HUDSON

deS. Childs, Ralph. "Phantom Ships of the Northeast Coast of North America." *New York Folklore Quarterly* V, no. 2 (Summer 1949).

Irving, Washington. "The Storm-Ship." *Bracebridge Hall*. First published in 1822. Accessed from Telelib.com April 12, 2015. http://www.telelib.com/authors/I/IrvingWashington/prose/bracebridgehallvol2/bracebridgehallv2022.html.

24. THE CURSED GHOST OF ALICE VAN DER VEER

Farnsworth, Cheri. *Haunted Hudson Valley: Ghosts and Strange Phenomena of New York's Sleepy Hollow Country*. Mechanicsburg, PA: Stackpole Books, 2010. Accessed on Google Books, April 13, 2015. https://books.google.com/books/about/Haunted_Hudson_Valley.html?id=zAIKsNfDdv0C.

Linedecker, Cliff. "Grieving Ghost Hunts for Her Dead Lover." *Weekly World News*, June 30, 1981. Accessed April 13, 2015. https://books
.google.com/books?id=1e8DAAAAMBAJ&pg=PA20&lpg=PA20&
dq=Alice+Van+der+Veer+Union+College&source=bl&ots=
r3vTVBX52Z&sig=vtVC8Pcog-rFiSTzE1gCOcHRXrI&hl=en&sa=X&ei
=gekrVbbDFMu8ggT4zILoDw&ved=0CDYQ6AEwBA#v=onepage&
q=Alice%20Van%20der%20Veer%20Union%20College&f=false.

Nilsson, B. A. "Ghost at Stake." *Words and Music*. October 31, 2012. Reposted from *Metroland Magazine*, October 27, 1988. Accessed April 13, 2015. http://banilsson.blogspot.com/2012/10/ghost-at-stake.html.

Shaw, James G., Jr. "Union College Ghost." *New York Folklore Quarterly* II, no. 2 (May 1946): 137–38.

"Spirit in the Night: A Ghost (Story) Haunts Jackson's Garden." Union College, October 30, 2014. Accessed April 13, 2015. http://
www.union.edu/news/stories/2014/10/spirit-in-the-night-a-ghost
-story-haunts-jacksons-garden.php.

25. POLITICS AND PAINTED POULTRY

Carrasquillo, Adrian. "The NYC City Council Speaker Frontrunner Is Being Sued for Allegedly Putting a Santeria Curse on an Opponent." BuzzFeed News, January 6, 2014. Accessed April 13, 2015. http://
www.buzzfeed.com/adriancarrasquillo/the-nyc-city-council-speaker
-frontrunner-is-being-sued-for-a#.qt8rJz2PB.

Duncan, Cynthia, PhD. "Osun, the Ever-Vigilant Sentry." AboutSanteria.com. Accessed April 13, 2015. http://www.
aboutsanteria.com/osun.html.

Duncan, Cynthia, PhD. Personal interview by email, April 13, 2015.

Goodwin, Gwen. "News Release on *Gwen Goodwin v. Melissa Mark-Viverito and Eastside Managers' Associates, Inc.*" Melissawatch.com, January 2, 2014. Accessed April 13, 2015. http://melissawatch.com/vC.html.

Gwen Goodwin, Plaintiff v. Melissa Mark-Viverito, and Eastside Managers' Associates, Inc. Defendants. Lawsuit filed in New York State Supreme Court, January 2, 2014. http://www.scribd.com/doc/195837129/GWEN-GOODWIN-Plaintiff-V-MELISSA-MARK-VIVERITO-and-EASTSIDE-MANAGERS-ASSOCIATES-INC-Defendants.

Marsh, Julia. "Loser Pol: Rival Put a Caribbean Hex on Me." *New York Post,* January 4, 2014. Accessed April 13, 2015. http://nypost.com/2014/01/04/loser-pol-rival-mark-viverito-put-a-curse-on-me.

@MMViverito on Twitter.com, January 4, 2014. Accessed April 13, 2015.

"New York City Councilwoman Accused in Lawsuit of Putting Voodoo Curse on Former Political Rival." *Fox News Latino,* January 6, 2014. Accessed April 13, 2015. http://latino.foxnews.com/latino/politics/2014/01/06/new-york-city-councilwoman-accused-in-lawsuit-putting-voodoo-curse-on-former.

Shango, Reverend Dr. Ekun Dayo Oni. "What Is the Difference between Voodoo, Hoodoo and Santeria?" SanteriaChurch.org, July 21, 2012. Accessed April 13, 2015. http://santeriachurch.org/what-is-the-difference-between-voodoo-hoodoo-and-santeria.

ACKNOWLEDGMENTS

Writing some books can be a solitary enterprise, but in the case of *Cursed in New York*, it took an entire state to make a book. I began my research by reaching out to the town historians in every region of the state, and I was amazed at the generosity they showed me with their time and resources. In particular, I must thank Cynthia Van Ness at the Buffalo History Museum; Judith Rundell, a volunteer at the Greene County Historical Society; Ron Cary, deputy Niagara County historian; Peter Schaaphok, historian of the town of Petersburgh; Eleanor R. Siliman, historian of Stueben County; Kaitlin Morton-Bentley, assistant curator of the Schenectady County Historical Society; Anne Gordon, Ulster County historian; Mark Slosek, Oswego County historian; and Richard Forliano, historian of the town of Eastchester.

Many people made themselves available for interviews or provided me with additional information by email. I am grateful to J. C. Anderson of Port City Paranormal; Cynthia Duncan of Santeria.com; Jenny Kellner, assistant director of communications for the New York Racing Association; Larry Smith, coordinator of tours and collections at Hyde Hall; and especially J. Dennis Petimezas, president of Watchmakers Diamonds and Jewelry, Inc., in Johnstown, Pennsylvania, for his willingness to participate in telling the whole story of the Black Orlov—and for his enthusiasm for the project.

It is always a pleasure to work with the people at the Globe Pequot Press. I must thank Amy Lyons, Jessie Shiers, Patricia Stevenson, and the rest of the team for everything we do together to create such beautiful books.

Regina Ryan, my agent for nearly ten years, is always available for my questions, concerns, and crises, and I so appreciate everything she does to keep my writing career so full and exciting.

To all the friends who support Nic and me as we work together to create our books, I cannot thank you all enough for opening your doors and your hearts to us. To Ken Horowitz, Rose-Anne Moore,

Martin Winer, Martha and Peter Schermerhorn, Ruth Watson and John King, Lorraine Woerner-MacGowan, and Kristen Kessler, I thank you all once again for being part of our adventures.

Finally, to Nic Minetor, my husband of twenty-five years, whose photos came together for the cover of this book and who is at my side through every journey, I love you and the life we have built together. God bless you and *ken-a-hora*!

INDEX

Huffman, Felicity, 110
Hyde Hall, 113–19; Ann Cooper
    Hyde forced to leave, 116–17;
    Ann Cooper Hyde haunting,
    118–19; construction of, 115, 116;
    curse origin and existence, 117–
    19; environs of, 113–14; family
    life/strife at, 115–17; origins and
    grandeur, 114; today, 114

Igneri, David, 18–19
immigrants: Astor Opera House riot/
    deaths and, 24–27; Irish, Mamie
    O'Rourke curse and, 37; "The
    Sidewalks of New York" and, 33
Indian burial grounds: Amityville
    curse and, 9–10; anti-retaliation
    laws for disturbing, 8; Buffalo
    curse and, 5–6; Chicago Cubs/
    Wrigley Field curse and, 8–9;
    curses from beyond the grave,
    8; disturbing, impact of, 7–8;
    federal act protecting, 11; Miami
    Dolphins curse and, 8; movies
    and, 10–11; Ralph Wilson
    Stadium and, 5, 6
Iroquois, 6, 8, 79
Irving, Washington, 161–63, 164–65
Isaac G. Jenkins (schooner), 50–51
Isabat al-'ayn, 1
Ivanovs, Janis, 71

James I, King of England, 22–23, 24
Jefferson, Thomas, 91, 94
Johnson, Sir William, 78

Kander, John, 31
Kellner, Jenny, 35–36

Kenny, Henry, 105
Kilpatrick, General John Reed, 53
King, Stephen, 10
Korper, George, 105

Ladue, Mlle., 101
Lake Ronkonkoma, 13–20;
    "bottomless" depths explained,
    15–16; historical attractiveness
    of, 14–15; lifeguard on deaths
    in, 18–19; location of, 14;
    men drowning in, 15, 18–20;
    overview of curse, 13–14
*Lake Ronkonkoma in History and
    Legend, the Princess, Curse, and Other
    Stories: A Lifeguard's View* (Igneri),
    18–19
Lansing, Judge John, 92–93, 94
La Salle, Robert de, 74, 75–77
Lawlor, Charles, 31, 32–33
lawsuit, political hex accusations,
    173–75, 177–78
Levy, Marv, 61
Lewiston, New York, 78
Liebman, Bennett, 34–35
Das Lied von der Erde (Mahler), 69–70
Lincoln, Abraham, 24
Livingston, Henry Brockholst, 90,
    91, 93, 95
logical fallacies, 4
Louis XIV, King of France, 98
Louis XV, King of France, 98
Louis XVI, King of France, 99
Lowinger, Aaron, 5, 6
Lutz family, 9–10

Macbeth. See The Tragedy of Macbeth
Macready, William Charles, 25–26

ninth symphony, curse of, 67–71; broken, 70–71; composers' deaths and, 68; Gustav Mahler and, 67–70

O'Dell, Nancy, 110
Onondaga, New York. *See* Thirteen Curves legend
Open Space Institute (OSI), 126
O'Rourke, Mamie, 33, 35, 36–37, 38
Orr, Bobby, 57
Osuna, Ric, 10

Pallotta, Thomasina, 129
Paranormal State (TV show), 41, 42, 45
Paris, Jan W., 105, 107
Parker, Arthur C., 6
Parker, Graham, 151
The Penguin Book of Witches, 145
Petimezas, J. Dennis, 109–11
Petke, Mike, 150, 151
Pet Sematary (King), 10
phantom ships, 161–65
Phillips, Robin, 28
Phillips, Wade, 64
Pierce, Frederic, 159
Pitau, Sieur, 98
Pittsburgh Penguins, 57
Plummer, Christopher, 27, 28–29
Poltergeist (film), 10
Port City Paranormal, 42, 44. *See also* Anderson, Doug; Anderson, Jane
Prince Hall Grand Lodge of New York, 125–26

Ralph Wilson Stadium, 5, 6
Real Quiet, 32

Ring, Catharine: cursing Hamilton, 93; Elma Sands' disappearance/murder and, 88–89, 92; later years, 95; relationship to Elma Sands, 87
Ring, Elias, 89, 90, 92, 95
Ronkonkoma: forbidden love for Birdsall, 13–14, 16–17; taking own life, 17–18. *See also* Lake Ronkonkoma
Roosevelt, Theodore, 60
rooster, religious significance of, 175, 176–77
Rorke, Mamie. *See* O'Rourke, Mamie
Rosen, Lawrence, 7
Rote, Mary, 40
Rubbra, Edmund, 71

Sabir, Abu, 101
Sands, Elma: body found in Manhattan Well, 89–90; curse following death of, 93–95; defense dream team and trial, 90–93; disappearance of, 88–90; overview, 87–88; relationship to Catharine Ring, 87. *See also* Burr, Aaron; Hamilton, Alexander; Ring, Catharine; Weeks, Levi
Santeria, 175–77
Schall, Thomas, 28–29
Schoenberg, Arnold, 67
Schubert, Franz, 68
Seattle Slew, 34, 36
Secretariat, 34, 36
Segerstam, Leif, 71
Seneca Indians, 6, 74–75, 76, 77–79
Setauket (Seatallcott), witchcraft trial in, 143–45

ABOUT THE AUTHOR

A lifelong resident of Rochester, New York, **Randi Minetor** has written twenty-seven books for the Globe Pequot Press, ranging from national park travel to American history to the best day hikes in upstate New York. Her books about New York State include five books in the *Best Easy Day Hikes* series, covering Rochester, Buffalo, Syracuse, Albany, and the Hudson River Valley; *Scenic Routes & Byways New York*; and *Hiking Waterfalls in New York*, all of which feature photos by her husband, Nic Minetor. She recently published *Day Trips: Hudson River Valley*. Randi's books on historic cities include four in the new *Historical Tours* series, on Gettysburg; Fredericksburg; Washington, DC; and the New York City immigrant experience. She and Nic also worked together on the bestselling *Backyard Birding: A Guide to Attracting and Identifying Birds*. Randi runs a successful media relations and writing business in Rochester with clients throughout the northeast region.